APPRENTICING
Jesus

THE FOUNDATION

This is one of my favorite books. It explores what it really looks like to get past doctrine & theology & follow Jesus as an example in how to live life, creating an existence & relationships that are purposeful & vibrant. I hope you enjoy it!

Merry Christmas!

MacKenzie, Andy, Peyton & Sloane

Apprenticing Jesus: The Foundation
Copyright © 2021 by Kris Kile

Visit the author's website at kriskile.com to sign up for his newsletter and to learn more about *Apprenticing Jesus* series and his transformative courses.

ISBN 978-1-945606-00-7
Published by Transform Publishing

Typesetting and Cover Design by FormattingExperts.com

FREE ADDITIONAL APPRENTICING JESUS RESOURCES

You can gain access to ten 10-minute videos with me introducing each chapter. It is an excellent enhancement to your *Apprenticing Jesus* study experience. In each video I explore the theme for that chapter.

To access these videos, visit:
https://KrisKile.com/ApprenticingJesusVideos

CONTENTS

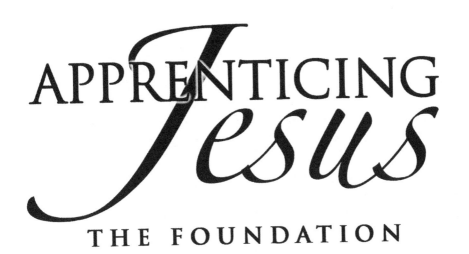

APPRENTICING *Jesus*

THE FOUNDATION

KRIS KILE

CHAPTER I

YOUR RESPONSE TO THE INVITATION OF A LIFETIME

I grew up in the church, attending church three times a week on most weeks from as early as I can remember through high school. I continued to learn about God and Jesus throughout college and beyond, and yet, I did not become fascinated with the life of Jesus on earth and the message he embodied until well into my adulthood, in my early fifties.

After thousands of hours studying scripture over my life until then, I had no real sense of Jesus's mission on earth. Of course, I knew all the answers I had been taught: he was the perfect sacrifice, and he came to make God accessible to us in the flesh. Essentially, he was a means to an end; the end being salvation for mankind.

Jesus seemed pretty distant to me, worthy of worship, far more than worthy of understanding and following. It almost seemed like the main thing about Jesus was his accomplishments relative to salvation and what we have as a result of his being around.

Then, I read Dallas Willard's book, *The Divine Conspiracy*, and it launched me into an entirely new consideration of Jesus as a personal mentor who has real life answers to real life issues, who had piercing insights that bypassed all convoluted ideologies that promise much but don't deliver in a way I had desired.

What is fascinating is that Jesus never asked us to worship him—not once. But he did ask us to *follow* him in Matthew 16:24 and on other occasions in the Gospels. Following, or apprenticing, is a different "game" than worshipping. Am I saying we should not worship Jesus or that he is not worthy of worship? I would never suggest that. I am only saying he never once asked us to do so. Yet, he definitely focused on inviting people to follow him.

Whether you currently believe Jesus is the son of God or not, his invitation above still stands… an invitation to follow him. To apprentice to him.

1

An apprentice is one who is learning by practical experience under a skilled practitioner's trade, art, or calling.

This study, *Apprenticing Jesus: The Foundation*, is a consideration of what life can be if you are serious about Jesus's words and example and make them a guide for your life. It is about practicing life the way Jesus practiced life, according to his words and his example.

Perhaps you're wondering, "So what's with all of this apprenticeship talk? What is the relevance of Jesus today in our confused and chaotic world?"

Consider what Jesus said about himself. He said in John 14:6, "I am the way, the truth, and the life." When you look at his entire statement in context, he amps up the ante even further:

Jesus said, "I am the Road, also the Truth, also the Life. No one gets to the Father apart from me. If you really knew me, you would know my Father as well. From now on, you do know him. You've even seen him!" (John 14:6–7, MSG)

This journey we are about to embark upon is designed to identify Jesus's key disciplines, practices, and distinctions and to embody them in a powerfully new and fresh way. Jesus promised that those who follow him will know fullness of life—they will *really* live. In a community of transformative love, they will carry out their lives in direct relationship with God and each other.

Jesus is a master teacher who is inviting us to mentor under him to create the greatest possible impact and experience of living. That really is good news! Jesus's message is just as relevant today as it was when he first gave it, and the opportunity to enter his apprenticeship into the fullness of life is still just as available.

Jesus's plan for his first followers was to make them his disciples—what we today might call apprentices. They got to learn firsthand from the Master how to live.

Today, when focusing primarily on the afterlife and the celestial heavens as the big benefit of Christianity, we have missed the reality that Jesus is available *here and now* to teach us how to live our actual, everyday lives as we are being transformed to be more like him. The

2

same opportunity to learn from the Master is extended to us many centuries later.

We are invited to become Jesus's apprentices in order to learn to live in the eternal, undying life of God himself, right here and now in the context of our everyday lives. This is *really* good news indeed. I'm not talking so much about what you are advocating for other people do in their lives. This is not a "virtue signaling" world I am inviting you into. Quite the contrary. I am talking about how you show up in your everyday life. I am talking about a new way to own your life, to own what is possible for you with others…to focus on the results you are producing with others and the impact you are having.

There were people in Jesus's day who focused primarily on telling others how they should act. They were the Pharisees and Sadducees—the religious leaders of his day. He offered a different path than they did, and they hated him for it. Jesus's path tends to subvert hypocrisy and arrogance and replace it with humility, clarity of purpose, and love.

Jesus is someone to actually imitate and not just to collectively worship. This has rarely been the norm or practice of most Christians. When you are apprenticed to Jesus, the emphasis is on practice over theory, or orthopraxy over orthodoxy. Orthodoxy teaches us the theoretical importance of love. Orthopraxy helps us learn *how* to love.

As apprentices of Jesus, love and action become more important than intellect or speculative truth. The intent of this study is to focus on the disciplines and practices that enable us to grow in our capacity to love and to embrace goodness as followers and apprentices of Jesus.

WHOSE DISCIPLE ARE YOU?

Who teaches you? Whose disciple are you? Honestly think about this. One thing is sure: you are somebody's disciple. You learned how to live from somebody else. There are no exceptions to this, for human beings are the kind of creatures who have to learn and keep learning from others how to live. It is how we are made.

Disciples, as we are defining it, are personal followers of Jesus, committed to be and do what Jesus instructs them to be and do. Disciples are committed to living their lives as Jesus would live them if he were they.

But in a general sense, we have all been discipled by many, many other people. Anyone who has influenced and impacted you has had a discipling role. That includes parents, teachers, siblings, those who inspired you, and those who disappointed and betrayed you. Your friends, extended family, siblings, peers—they have all had a discipling effect on you.

To consider all who have impacted your life is revealing, especially when you realize this impact spreads beyond those you have personally interacted with. It includes those you consciously or unconsciously admire or aspire to be like—celebrities, heroes, sports figures, philosophers, politicians, religious leaders, musicians, and more. It also includes those who lived long ago whose ideas you now embrace—either consciously or unconsciously. Those who shaped the culture you live in, those who influenced the collective beliefs about "the way it is" where you live as well as the people with whom you associate.

Much of the residue of all these influences operates in our lives unconsciously, below the radar, like the software of our lives that runs in the backgrounds of our minds. It accomplishes many functions, from influencing what you think is wanted or needed in any situation to compensating for what you think is lacking in you or others. You act on the hundreds (or maybe thousands?) of assumptions, assessments, judgments, and opinions that make up the sum total of your belief systems and psyche. They define how you see reality and what you believe to be possible.

You already are a disciple. The question is, whose? And are you interested in being re-discipled by the Master of life—to become an apprentice of Jesus? The question bears serious scrutiny, because his plan for life cuts against the grain of popular culture and most of the discipling influences we have had in our lives.

To be an apprentice of Jesus is to believe in "the impossible" (Ephesians 3:20). Through Christ, God tells us he can do exceedingly, abundantly above anything we ask or think. This invitation is designed to transform the limiting conversations we have about ourselves, others, and life.

Following Jesus, then, requires a willingness to take yourself on and challenge the assumptions you currently live in. When we do this, an opening for transformation is possible.

4

Transformation is a radical concept. It means to become brand-new, to experience a substantive change in form and character. The Greek word we translate "transformed" is also the word from which we get "metamorphosis", the process by which a caterpillar is changed into a butterfly. It is a complete change of form, character, and substance. That degree of change will certainly be recognizable by others as well as yourself. That is God's desire for you. This is your opportunity to embrace it.

BEING MENTORED BY JESUS

Jesus's mentorship comes to us in several ways:

- His words and actions during his three-year ministry on earth.
- His accomplishments throughout history with his followers.
- His active personal interactions today with his disciples.

Yes, Jesus is still at hand and actively building his kingdom, and he invites you to join his community of transformative love. He gives you not just a promise of being with him in a future eternity but of entering the life of God here and now. Some think they can ignore the life he offers us in this world and in our time and say, "Oh, well, I'll just wait till I get to heaven to experience God." That is clearly *not* what Jesus had in mind.

The invitation to apprentice with Jesus is not for the faint of heart. It is not the path of least resistance. It is at times unpredictable. It can destabilize your inherent desire for comfort and certainty.

This journey is also full of paradox and mystery. It is not about mastering information, techniques, or formulas. It is about a relationship with the Master of life, apprenticing yourself to him as your mentor. This journey is not about comfort. Rather than resisting the inherent pain and suffering of life, you will be invited to engage it in a new way, with the possibility of experiencing the joy on the other side.

You will be invited to embrace hope in the face of despair, love in the face of hurt, and faith in the face of uncertainty. You will be invited to be curious rather than certain, to listen more than you advise, to replace judgment with empathy and compassion. You will be invited to respond to hurtfulness with kindness and harshness with gentleness. This, obviously, is hard work. But it is also genuinely transformative work. The invitation is to embrace unprecedented transformation, faith that overcomes doubt and cynicism, hope that overcomes despair, and love that casts out all fear.

THE RESULTS OF APPRENTICING WITH JESUS

The life to which Jesus has invited us is the ultimate journey. It is designed to:

- Transform what you see as possible in your life and with others
- Introduce an appreciation for paradox and mystery
- Enthrall you with the realization of the gift you have been given
- Empower you with the reality of the gift you are for others

Perhaps this all seems outlandish to you. Perhaps it looks interesting but impossible. But what if, as God has promised, it is possible? Why not keep an open mind and try it? Perhaps we will be surprised, as so many have before us. God is certainly capable of surprising us. He promises us the possibility of transformation in Romans 12:2. The heart of transformation is breaking through what looks impossible to the place of having it happen.

HOW TO USE THIS STUDY

This study aims to take you on a journey of transformation through apprenticing with Jesus. God promises the unequivocal *possibility* of transformation. He does not, however, promise its *inevitability*. It takes rigorous, intentional, diligent, disciplined participation in order for this transformation to manifest itself in your life on a consistent basis.

My view is that any study of Christ-likeness founded on techniques, formulas, or programs will fail. What Jesus offers us are disciplines and practices that are catalyzed and made transformational through radical dependency and trust. *This is because following Jesus is a relationship.* It can't be learned from a manual. It is built on the foundation of our learning to rest and abide in God's presence, goodness, grace, mercy, and forgiveness.

This study is established through practical ways to abide in Jesus and to learn from him in the context of everyday life. This journey is not about arriving. "Arrival" is a deception of our self-help-focused culture. Our attempts at arrival usually smell of performance, control, and arrogance.

Henri Nouwen, a profound modern writer on spiritual growth, said this toward the end of his life:

> After many years of seeking to live a spiritual life, I still ask myself, "Where am I as a Christian? How far have I advanced? Do I love God more now than earlier in my life? Have I matured in faith since I started on the spiritual path?" Honestly, I don't know the answers to these questions. There are just as many reasons for pessimism as for optimism. Many of the real struggles of twenty or forty years ago are still very much with me. I am still searching for inner peace, for creative relationships with others, and for a deeper experience of God. And I have no way of knowing if the small psychological and spiritual changes during the past decades have made me more or less a spiritual person. In a society that overvalues progress, development, and personal achievement, the spiritual life becomes quite easily performance oriented. On what level am I now, and how do I move to the next one? When will I reach union with God? When will I experience illumination or enlightenment? Many great saints have described their religious experiences, and many lesser saints have systematized them into difference phases, levels or stages. These distinctions may be helpful for those who write books for instruction, but *it is of great importance that we leave the world of measurement behind when we speak about the life of the Spirit.*[1] (Emphasis mine.)

Rather than offering a magic bullet or the possibility of "arriving" somewhere so we can coast, this learning journey is designed to support you in making decisions to choose life and blessings rather than "death" or curses on a moment-by-moment basis (Deuteronomy 30:19). Scripture makes it clear that we get to choose afresh in each moment.

Thus, it's clear that, to quote a contemporary proverb, "it's all about the journey, not the destination."

I believe that Jesus intended us to live life to its fullest without fear of failure dictating our actions. The life to which he calls us is not a life free of mistakes, lived timidly in order to avoid stepping over the line.

Therefore, our primary focus will not be on what to do. It will be on how to discover and create a vision worthy of the gift of life you now enjoy and the eternal life you have been promised. It will be about engaging the tension between your current reality and that vision. It will be about eternal living in the present and into the future. It will be about courage and a willingness to take risks as you discover just how big a "game" God has laid out for you.

THE PRINCIPAL AIM

Throughout this study, our principal aim will be to plumb the bottomless depths of what it means to live, give, and experience love.

> A new command I give you: Love one another. As I have loved you, so you must love one another. By this everyone will know that you are my disciples, if you love one another. (John 13:34–35, NIV)

This was Jesus's command to his disciples shortly before his betrayal and crucifixion. Elsewhere, he summed up what it means to follow and honor God in the simplest yet most profound axiom ever uttered: "Love the Lord your God with everything and your neighbor as your own self" (Matthew 22:37–41).

Jesus returns to this central theme again and again: *agape love, God's unconditional love, is the central and distinguishing characteristic of those who follow Jesus.* Not knowledge, not power, not giftedness, not faith, not generosity, and not personal sacrifice. Love. The church has often made following Jesus about mastering knowledge, managing sin, or trying to be good. Where love is present, these things take care of themselves.

We often don't believe, as Scripture tells us, that "Love never fails." We don't believe it because we accept the lies told by our culture, specifically the lie that if we don't take care of our own selves, first and foremost, there won't be enough love to go around. Taking care of yourself is important. But what gets lost in that equation is this: as we are exercising self-care, we are also called to engage others with care and love. One does not have to perfect the former in order to embrace the latter. We are to engage both disciplines simultaneously.

Living love is the highest aim of life. The pursuit of love is the ultimate, glorious, divine struggle. Consider this: if those of us who call ourselves followers of Jesus (or "Christians" or "believers") are known collectively for anything other than our transformational expressions of love, then we have gone astray. Whenever we despair of the possibility of love (with a spouse, friend, family member, acquaintance, or enemy), God is calling us into deeper waters, to discover a new expression of love we have not yet experienced and given.

This study, then, is designed to support your pursuit of living a depth of love that never fails. We will see this most clearly in how we love our neighbors, brothers, and sisters—those closest to us and those near us.

> If someone says, "I love God," and hates his brother, he is a liar; for he who does not love his brother whom he has seen, how can he love God whom he has not seen? And this commandment we have from him: that he who loves God must love his brother also. (1 John 4:20–21, NKJV)

These verses strip any pretense away. They are sobering—and an amazing declaration of possibility. Imagine the possibility of viewing each opportunity of loving another as an opportunity to love and know God! Imagine Jesus teaching us to love others and, in the process, drawing us closer to God.

How do we seek and experience this kind of transformed life in a sustainable way? That is the real question. How do we get this reality into our daily lives? We have great hope, for the invitation is to come alongside the Master of love, allowing him to guide us, be with us, and lead us down this path.

HOW EACH WEEK'S JOURNEY WORKS

This journey is designed to generate the most value within a small group environment. Ideally, the small group will meet once per week for two hours, but some groups have done this study with weekly meetings ranging from one hour to three hours. And, of course, you can also use this as an individual study.

Each chapter will focus on a specific topic to be considered and applied throughout the following week. The chapter will start with a few pages of thoughts for you to read and consider as your main areas of focus and attention. At the end of each chapter, you will be given some "daily" contemplative prayer topics for that week. They are designed to more fully develop that week's themes both in thought and practice.

These daily contemplation topics are designed to introduce some very powerful transformative spiritual disciplines, such as silence, solitude, contemplation, and contemplative prayer. Over the course of this eight-week study, I will gradually unfold details regarding these disciplines and also what I call "awakening prayer."

In your small group, you will have the opportunity to share what you are learning and noticing and receive input and feedback from others as you all live this process together. Your commitment to openness, honesty, authenticity, and vulnerability will accelerate the pace of your growth.

There are three main elements of interaction included in this process. They are: (1) the material itself and your considerations of it in application to your life, (2) the daily practice of spiritual disciplines and prayer, and (3) the commitment to walk this out with others, engaging each other with a deep commitment to authenticity.

If you engage all three elements on a consistent basis, you will maximize the experience and impact of this study. If you simply read the material and skip steps 2 and 3, you will diminish the impact it can have on your life. If you do not have a small group to walk alongside you, you can enlist a friend or two to go through the course with you. *Transformation is designed to be lived out in community.* Engaging this in community will make a big difference.

HOW TO GET THE MOST OUT OF THIS STUDY

This can be summed up in two words: *full participation.*

Full participation means being fully engaged, open, honest, vulnerable, and willing to "live in the question." Rather than quickly skipping through your questions and considerations, be willing to look beyond your current set of assumptions, assessments, judgments, opinions, and beliefs about yourself, others, and life. Be willing to consider and own your contribution to breakdowns in your life rather than minimizing and dismissing them.

Be willing to openly ponder, reflect, and observe where an inquiry leads you—consider it an "ongoing inquiry." Marinate in the question. Be open. Be curious. This mindset is essential. The practice of nonjudgmentally, reflectively observing yourself and what makes you tick, rather than simply being caught up in your own responses without really considering or noticing them, is a fundamental transformational discipline.

At the same time, notice what you resist and the ways you avoid. This might look like impatience, being quick to dismiss an idea as something you already know or something not worth your time, joking, minimizing, making excuse, intellectualizing—the list goes on and on. When these responses come up for you, choose to release them, be courageous, and participate fully. Take the posture of a learner, not a knower.

Full participation also includes a deep commitment to action. There is a vast difference between knowing information and living it.

Finally, remember that patience is a virtue. This is a journey for the long-term—a journey of apprenticeship that will extend far beyond the final pages of this book. Jesus's way takes time. Be patient with yourself, and give yourself time to learn, grow, and mature.

WRITE OUT A COMPELLING VISION

Proverbs 29:18a declares, "Where there is no vision, the people perish" (KJV). In this verse, the word "perish" can also be translated "are naked" or "wander aimlessly." Creating a compelling, practical vision will be a big boost to your participation in this course. And the more specifically grounded the vision is in practical aspects of your life, the more useful and powerful it will be.

Consider the key areas of your life and relationships that you desire to transform. Perhaps these areas are going okay but are not where you desire them to be. Perhaps some areas in your life are in breakdown mode, and you deeply desire to create new possibilities in them.

The more specifically you ground your participation in this study to real life issues that are challenging you, the more you will learn and the more value you will generate through your participation.

The overall focus of our efforts is apprenticing with Jesus. But becoming an apprentice of Jesus does not mean merely acquiring new knowledge. It means transforming your way of being—the way you show up in the world, your attitudes and actions and assumptions and belief systems—such that you become a living, walking representation of Jesus's love and life in the present tense.

Being an apprentice of Jesus leads to very practical shifts in being, transforming who you are with and for others. These transformational shifts can take you from resentment to gratitude, from resignation to hope, from fear to love, from apathy to care, from isolation to connection.

This week, take the opportunity to start developing a vision statement for the time and effort you are investing in this study's growth process. Think about areas of your life and relationships where you are currently resigned, or settling, or experiencing disappointment, loss, despair, or resentment. We all have these challenges to grapple with. Yet as Jesus's apprentices, we get to tackle these areas with renewed hope, vigor, and resources to create new possibilities and results. Write down the change you hope to see in these areas as a result of your apprenticeship.

For example, look to the relationships that mean the most to you. Consider your spouse, your children, your immediate family, your close friends. What about work relationships or extended family? You can focus on different areas of vision with them, such as being committed to creating a deeper experience of love through being patient instead of reactive, calm instead of angry, curious instead of defensive, grateful instead of resentful, hopeful instead of despairing. Think about the practical areas of your life where you desire deeper connection or a more fulfilling experience of living with God and others. Think through the specifics of what you are willing to commit to generating, whether it be love, joy, peace, passion, wonderment, connection, trust, patience, or something else.

To do so will require you to let go of any idealized views of how well you are doing and take a genuine look at your current reality. For example, when considering a relationship you are not satisfied with, shift off of focusing on *them* and what you think they are or are not doing right. Instead, focus on the parts of what *you* are contributing to the relationship that are contributing to the breakdown. God's transformative work within you is not dependent on those around you, even those closest to you. It depends on *your* willingness to discipline yourself in his ways.

As an example, if part of my vision is growing a deeper love relationship with my wife, Katie, I can choose to pay attention to where I have lingering resentments, disappointments, or apathy toward her—no matter how small or seemingly tolerable they are. These are big openings for new possibility if I am willing to notice them, pursue an increased awareness of why I am indulging them, and create a vision for what I desire with my wife in place of them. I can choose to pursue new ground with her in the areas of vulnerability, trust, intimacy, and connection. I can notice when I tend to withhold the conversations I have in my mind about our relationship—the ones I avoid having out loud. A fear of vulnerability—being rejected or misunderstood—can get in the way of openness and intimacy. For me, this fear of vulnerability is usually rooted in a lack of trust that God will be with me no matter what. When I indulge this fear, I rob us of the opportunity to deepen our relationship and express love for each other.

There is a tension in honestly considering your current reality when it is not close to matching your vision. But being willing to enter that tension, release judgment for yourself and others, and wade into the dynamics of your current reality is the path to freedom. *The path to transformation is through.*

You can also include in your vision statement areas of your life where you desire to interrupt attitudes and actions that are not in alignment with the vision of life Jesus unfolded in the Gospels. These could include overcoming hurtful attitudes and actions, like anger and contempt, or overcoming addictions or harmful habits and replacing them with life-giving ways of being.

If you build a vibrant vision for who you are committed to be with others, that vision can be powerful enough to pull you through the challenges of genuine transformation. It will call on you to continually "go again" while pressing into God's provision as you walk this path of discipline and obedience.

Your vision statement can include any facet of your life. It can include your professional life, community commitments, church and ministry commitments, or health and education. Feel free to include specifics in these areas also, and be specific about the new ground you are committing to taking.

As you move forward in the study, consider every principle, distinction, discipline, and practice covered in relation to the areas of focus in your vision statement. The daily prayer topics throughout are designed to support you in putting your vision into action. *Your life is a gift, not only to you, but also to others.* You are called to give the gift that you are. This course is an opportunity to discover the gift that you are for others in a new and fresh way, with clarity and intentionality, as you take action on a clear vision.

Spend this week developing a vision statement. Two topics have been provided for this purpose.

ABOUT SPIRITUAL PRACTICES

In this study, at the end of each chapter you will find topics to focus on during the week. Some chapters have a couple *Spiritual Practice* topics for that week and other chapters have several *Spiritual Practice* topics for that week. These topics are each designed to be a focus for a day.

TOPIC 1: DEVELOPING A COMPELLING VISION

Today, start considering your vision for this journey:

- What outcomes are you interested in creating?
- What areas of your life do you desire to create newness in?
- What important relationships do you desire to take new ground in?

These considerations are the beginning of the development of a compelling vision. We will take some time to fully flesh this out. Today, I am asking you to start your considerations regarding it.

VISION FOCUS:

Name at least one important relationship you are considering engaging as a part of your vision for this *Apprenticing Jesus* study. If you have more than one relationship that you desire to improve and create newness in, write them all down for now. You can hone it down in the coming weeks.

Name at least one important area of your life that you are interested in changing, growing in, or overcoming obstacles in.

As you pray and as you go through your day, consider these areas and ask God to reveal to you other areas of importance that you may not be considering. Be open to gaining clarity regarding what you are willing to commit to accomplish in your life over the next eight weeks.

DAILY SCRIPTURE

Lamentations 3:40: "Let us examine our ways and test them, and let us return to the Lord." (NIV)

TOPIC 2: BUILDING A COMPELLING VISION

Today, continue to contemplate and write out your vision for this journey we are on together during this study. Don't be concerned with whether it is perfect or not. Start writing down what is occurring to you and what you are identifying regarding your vision. Just write down what is true for you right now.

VISION FOCUS:

Build off of your considerations from regarding the relationships and areas of your life you are committed to transforming. You will have time to further hone them in the next chapter.

DAILY SCRIPTURE

Romans 12:2: "And do not be conformed to this world, but be transformed by the renewing of your mind, that you may prove what is that good and acceptable and perfect will of God" (NIV).

CHAPTER 2

BEGINNING STEPS AS AN APPRENTICE

The more I study the Gospels, the more amazed I am at Jesus's audacity in calling us as his apprentices. Before we consider the entry-level commitment he has invited us into, I have a request of you: Set aside whatever you associate with or however you define the word "repentance."

The word "repentance" can mean very different things to each person. Based on some experiences, the word is infused with shame and judgment.

Instead of shame and judgement, consider repentance as an exhilarating invitation to possibility in your life. It literally means to change your mind and purpose for the better. In essence, it is an invitation to change the trajectory of your life so that it aligns with the life Jesus describes in the Gospels.

ENGAGING YOUR VISION

As you explore the concept of repentance in this week's readings, apply it to your personal vision by giving serious thought to where you need a new start in your life and relationships.

A FRESH TAKE ON FIRST STEPS: REPENT!

In Matthew 3:2, John the Baptist prophesies the imminent coming of the Messiah with the words, "Repent, for the kingdom of heaven is at hand."

Matthew 4:17 says that from the time Jesus began to preach, he declared "Repent, for the kingdom of heaven is at hand." (ESV)

In Acts 2:37, on the day of Pentecost (after Jesus's crucifixion, resurrection, and ascension into heaven), after the outpouring of the Holy Spirit and Peter's sermon to those present, the crowds were cut to the heart and asked him, "What shall we do?"

Peter responded "Repent, every one of you, in the name of Jesus Christ for the forgiveness of your sins. And you will receive the gift of the Holy Spirit."

Are you noticing a trend here? When it comes to following Jesus, it seems pretty obvious that the first consideration and action to be taken is to repent. As stated earlier, repent literally means "to change." It means to change your mind and your heart. It involves more than adopting new ideas. It is transformational change—a substantive change in character.

Unfortunately, the word *repent* has a lot of baggage. Through the centuries, it has been utilized in many different contexts in Christian circles. For some of us, the word *repent* conjures up images of some wild preacher shouting shame, judgment, and recrimination to others from the sidewalk of a city, or from behind the pulpit. It seems that, in many ways, it has lost its power and efficacy in today's culture. Yet I believe this word, and the concept it communicates, has immense resource and meaning for us today.

Repentance is a huge invitation for growth, for possibility, and for more consistently experiencing love, connection, and goodness.

In Mark 1:14–19, Jesus began preaching the good news that the kingdom of God was at hand. He specifically invited those who were listening to respond to this reality with three actions—*repent, believe,* and follow. The first step was to commit to changing—to repent. Apprenticing Jesus is a never-ending commitment to change and growth.

REPENTANCE AS THE FOUNDATION OF TRANSFORMATION

Consider that the concept of repentance includes a commitment to intentionality, specific attitudes, ways of being, and specific actions. Jesus started with repentance because it is the foundation of transformation.

Genuine, sustainable transformation is a three-legged stool. Its three fundamental elements are renewing the mind, shifting the posture of the heart, and repentance. All three of these aspects are interconnected, but it is clear in Scripture that Jesus believed the beginning of the path to being part of the kingdom of heaven was repentance—a commitment and will to change. The invitation from Jesus here is for you to change.

It is not focused on you telling everyone else to change while ignoring and excusing where you miss the mark. This is about owning your life.

Repentance is not just a one-time action. It is an ongoing way of relating and living, with a deep commitment to staying the course on a new trajectory in life.

WHAT IS REPENTANCE?

One theology dictionary defines repentance as:

> *To change one's mind and purpose.* This change is always for the better and denotes a change of moral thought and reflection; not merely to repent of nor to forsake sin, but to change one's mind and apprehensions regarding it; hence, to repent in a moral and religious sense, with the feeling of remorse and sorrow … (in Latin, *resipisco*, to recover one's senses, come to a right understanding; and *resipiscentia*, the growing wise) … denotes to reform, to have a *genuine change of heart and life* from worse to better.[2]

A lifestyle of repentance is a lifestyle of becoming new. It means to live responsibly. Own your life. Own your impact. Account for where you miss the mark. Embrace compunction, contrition, and conversion. Adjust your direction when you go off course and start again, and again, and again, and again.

It is through God's mercy and forgiveness that we are enabled to go again. Our mercy and forgiveness for others keeps us in the game. Live your life in the context of relationship and community and remain mindful of your primary purpose of existence—to live love.

A lifestyle of repentance is the price of admission into experiencing life in the kingdom of heaven. Repentance is a posture of the heart, which is revealed by your life and relationships—your impact in its totality, including the good, the bad, and the ugly.

COMING TO REPENTANCE

Repentance is the result of three actions that have been lost to a degree over the course of church history. Understanding these actions brings clarity as to what genuine repentance involves and will enrich your awareness of what it means to live a lifestyle of repentance.

You may have heard some of these terms before. I ask you again to consider afresh what they mean. They are *compunction, contrition,* and *conversion*—all of which lead to repentance.

COMPUNCTION

Compunction is a stinging or puncturing of the conscience caused by awareness and regret for doing wrong or causing pain. It is from the Latin, *compungere*—to sting, to puncture.[3]

> Compunction involves a moment of awakening, the first glimmer of enlightenment, the dawning of a new day lived against a different horizon. St. John Cassian defines compunction as whatever can by God's grace waken our lukewarm and sleepy souls. This definition seems to envisage us living our spiritual lives in a slumberous state of half-wakefulness. The grace of compunction is the transition to a state of fuller awareness. The great difference between the saints and the rest of us is that they were spiritually awake more of the time than we are. They were alert to possibilities … We who stumble through life with many mistakes and omissions admire their saintly deeds but without necessarily realizing that perhaps we could imitate them more closely if our spiritual senses were not so drowsy.[4]

One of the great deterrents to embracing repentance today is our lack of awareness of the impact we are having on others and on ourselves. We become so absorbed in our own subjectivity, our own view of "how things are," and so focused on getting our needs met or what others are "doing wrong," that we lose all perspective on the impact we are generating through our attitudes and actions.

How can I repent of something I am unaware of, or deny, or minimize, or explain away, or blame on another?

Compunction has absolutely nothing to do with guilt. I am not talking about you feeling guilty about falling short. Guilt has no place with compunction or repentance. The reality is that guilt will lead you in the opposite direction of repentance. Guilt is disempowering. Compunction and repentance are life giving. Guilt is all about you. Compunction is all about the other. Guilt is narcissistic. Compunction is benevolent. Guilt leads to appeasement and excusing. Compunction leads to ownership, change, and engaging the other to create forgiveness and a new opening to engage.

Compunction is the beginning of awareness that can lead to a new orientation. It leads to a deeper spiritual awakening.

CONTRITION

In this road to repentance, after compunction, comes contrition. Contrition is the state of being remorseful and sorrowful for having done wrong.

Contrition is *not* about beating yourself up, judging yourself, or engaging in self-loathing or self-contempt. In fact, all of those are the opposite of true contrition. Self-contempt, guilt, and self-loathing are a preoccupation with self, and are an expression of selfishness—the opposite of love.

Rather, contrition is remorse and sorrow due to harm done *to another.* It is about the other, not about self. It is about my missing the mark (of love) with another and allowing the impact that miss had on the other to penetrate my heart, connecting with me both mentally and emotionally.

Contrition sets us on a completely different trajectory than self-judgment, guilt and condemnation.

CONVERSION

After contrition comes conversion. Conversion can be defined in several different ways. My use of conversion here is a *lifestyle* of repentance (rather than a one-off act). Conversion is the ongoing discipline of reorienting ourselves away from our self-serving emotional reactions, defense mechanisms, and fixations and toward actions that are virtuous and loving toward others.

Sometimes conversion is described as a vice-to-virtue conversion. Anger, pride, deceit, envy, avarice, anxiety, gluttony, lust, and sloth are all examples of vices. *Virtue* is moral excellence, a positive trait or quality valued as a foundation of principle and good moral being. It is the opposite of vice.[5] Humility, truthfulness, serenity, generosity, courage, sobriety, faith, hope, and love are examples of virtues.

Conversion means to turn around. It is about noticing when we are caught up in our failings or imperfections and then turning in trust toward God's grace and mercy. Through God's mercy we can move toward the true essence that God has created us to be.

WHAT IS SIN?

Sin is another word charged with historical meanings that vary greatly depending on your background. The word translated *sin* in biblical Greek is *hamartia*, which means to "miss the mark, to swerve from, to err."[6] In ancient Christianity, vices such as the ones listed above were considered significant sins—sins that impact the posture of the heart so that other failings and sins are produced by them.

It seems that in much of church culture today, sin is coupled tightly with shame and seen as something that needs to be "managed" or eliminated. Sin management is rooted in self focus and perfecting one's self. That is a fool's errand. You are never going to be perfect in this life. But the mindset of sin management presupposes that I am supposed to be without sin. So, when I miss the mark, I do what I can to hide my shame, just like Adam did in Genesis in the garden.

You are going to miss the mark. When you recognize it, that is an invitation to confess, to be honest, to embrace God's grace and mercy, to ask forgiveness, and, in that humility, to commit to going again. Sin management invites hiding, minimizing, avoiding, and lying. It is based on the impossible standard of projecting a life without sin. It is rooted in an impossibility and a lie. The fact is, we are going to miss the mark. The goal of having zero defects is a fool's hope.

The antidote to sin management is conversion...freely choosing to embrace the posture of the heart which leads to bad behavior and transforming the iniquity that came from the selfish posture of the heart. This is why conversion is a lifelong commitment. It embraces transparency, authenticity, honesty, and openness.

To the best of your ability, seek to separate the energy of shame from the areas where you feel you are captured by your failings or compulsions. Let's forge a new path that embraces God's mercy and grace. Seek to set a consistent new trajectory in the areas you have purposed in your vision.

HOW REPENTANCE LEADS TO RENEWAL

*Repentance embodies setting a new trajectory...of changing course...*of turning around to pursue the life Jesus unfolds for us in the Gospels. The trajectory set by repentance allows us to enter what the apostle Paul called newness of life. Repentance is a lifestyle of openness and authenticity. The need for it never goes away, because we are flawed and imperfect. Repentance is never about beating yourself up, as this only leads to a self-centered focus and despair without turning toward God. Repentance is born out of godly sorrow for missing the mark with God and others.

Repentance draws from a gratitude that permeates the depths of your soul—a gratitude born when we realize the immensity of the gift of grace and mercy God has bestowed upon us. This grace and mercy birthed his invitation to eternal living and his gift of a new birth. Joy and delight are born from this depth of gratitude.

Repentance draws from a deep humility—a humility that is born from gratitude for God's calling in your life. It draws from a realization that God has called you to be a unique gift to the world that no one else can replicate or duplicate. It is a realization that you were saved for a purpose. That your life is not your own. That you were bought with Jesus's sacrifice for a purpose.

Repentance draws from a deep desire to be a continual expression of love to others, God, and self. It is aware that loving the other is always about *impacting* the other with love. Loving God and loving others are the essence of the game of life (Luke 10:27).

Repentance results in trusting God. It trusts God to redeem the tragedies and losses of the past and to restore them. It trusts God to redeem and to restore the losses of the present—both those initiated by you and those initiated by others.

Repentance breeds a willingness to live responsibly in life, accounting for your life and considering the feedback others give you regarding your impact. It embraces the current reality of your life as your guide rather than relying on a fantasy view of life you wish were true. Repentance does the heavy lifting of owning your contribution and course-correcting whenever your current reality indicates that as a need.

Repentance embraces surrender. Surrender is about accepting the realities of your life, in the present moment, without resisting them. It is not resignation, condoning, agreeing with or capitulation. It is embracing the current reality to discover God's provision in it, even if it appears there could be none. Genuine surrender cannot happen without a trust that God is still in it and worthy of that trust. It is about embracing God as the provider of our salvation rather than trying to be our own savior.

Repentance is the motivation for doing the disciplined work of renewing the mind, which includes renewing your thought life, renewing the posture of your heart, and renewing the personal impact you are having on the world on a continual basis.

Repentance creates freedom and power as you embrace God's invitation to be the author of your life, in collaboration with him. It doesn't blame others, or God, or your circumstances, for the current status of your life. It fully embraces your responsibility before God for your life. Life has losses, tragedies and betrayals. We can't always control the circumstances we face. But, we can always control our response to these challenges. How you "show up" and respond in those circumstances in *your choice.* You are called to co-create your future with God. He is always there to guide and you are always responsible to own your life and be the author of your legacy, as you co-create it with God.

Without embracing repentance as a lifestyle, you probably won't be up for following the rigorous path of apprenticeship for the long haul. *But this is the true path to freedom and fulfillment. There is no other. This* **is** *the good life.*

RENEWING YOUR THOUGHT LIFE

The weapons we fight with are not the weapons of the world. On the contrary, they have divine power to demolish strongholds. We demolish arguments and every pretension that sets itself up against the knowledge of God, and we take captive every thought to make it obedient to Christ. (2 Corinthians 10:4–5, NIV)

Repentance means to change our minds, and in practical terms, that involves transforming and renewing our thought lives. The language in 2 Corinthians 10:4–5 is forceful. It implies high-energy intentionality. We demolish strongholds, demolish arguments and pretensions, and take thoughts captive. This is not the path of least resistance, and it does not necessarily come easily. But it is possible—it is doable!

DEMOLISHING STRONGHOLDS

The strongholds we build in our lives have a huge impact on how we react to events. A stronghold is initially a place of safety, but it can develop into a place of captivity. The Greek word in Scripture for "stronghold," taken literally, means a fortress. Strongholds are walls or fortresses we have built around beliefs and emotions to protect us from pain.

Strongholds are belief systems which operate throughout our lives to help us get through the inevitable disappointments, losses, betrayals, and challenges we face. We often build them unconsciously.

For example, a little girl who suffered sexual abuse from a man developed a belief that men can't be trusted and that she should always be wary around men. When she was young, that was important to follow, because it could help keep her safe from harm. Her belief became a stronghold—a place of safety. But that same belief system will continue to run in her unconscious and subconscious mind as an adult. And in that stage of life, it becomes a problem. This stronghold becomes a place of bondage—captivity. It can bind her and prevent her from developing trusting relationships with men. The point is not that this concern is invalid. Some men should not be trusted. The point is that this concern is operating unconsciously and is equally and indiscriminately applied to all.

When this now-woman applies her fear and suspicion to non-abusers, it creates mischief in her relationships. She is operating under unconscious assumptions about men that may not apply to them. The key is *awareness*—her awakening to how this fear operates in her. When it shows up, then, she can determine whether the fear is valid or just a haunting from her past.

27

Essentially, strongholds are survival-based living strategies that we all have. *Having* them is not the problem. *Relying* on them as the primary way to get through life is the problem.

Life with God requires that we identify those areas of our lives where we are living "in survival mode" and then transform—renew—those ways of relating. God has called us to thrive and flourish… not to merely survive. We can choose new ways of relating to others and caring for ourselves. The results of our lives are an indicator of which belief systems are guiding us.

If the results you are producing do not match your desires—your conscious intentions—then you can choose to identify your internal conversations that limit you and lead to lackluster results. You can identify the strongholds—survival-based, unhealthy ways of relating—and interrupt them. You can redesign these limiting beliefs. This requires trusting God and redesigning your beliefs and internal conversations from limiting to empowering and flourishing. This is a continual renewal process we are called to.

DEMOLISHING ARGUMENTS AND PRETENSIONS

The Message refers to bringing down "arguments and pretensions" as "tearing down barriers erected against the truth of God, fitting every loose thought and emotion and impulse into the structure of life shaped by Christ."

We all have the ability to rationalize and reason our way into justifying our behavior, no matter how outrageous or hurtful it is. Pretensions are elevated thoughts: inflated thoughts about ourselves, or any other aspect of life, which are contrary to the knowledge of God. We all tend to have inflated views of ourselves. Because of our good intentions, we ignore what we are actually producing in life, and defend our good intentions. This works against repentance and prevents us from changing our impact.

God is challenging us to get in touch with the current reality of what is actually happening in our lives and to get busy renewing our thought patterns that are out of sync with God's truth. We have an invitation to build new thought patterns that lead to transformed lives. Neuroscientists now know that humans can change their brains—they can build new neural pathways and establish new thought patterns. Scientists believed for decades that this was not possible for adults. It is nice to see science finally catch up with what God has been saying for a long time! In neuroscience terms, this ability to change our minds is called *neuroplasticity*.

When we interrupt stronghold-based thought patterns and renew them into brand-new thought patterns based on the truth of what God says, we generate an entirely new way of relating that has a powerful impact on our experience of living. Doing so requires discipline, consistency, and a willingness to go again and again, from a nonjudgmental, neutral, determined, and committed mind-set. This is the daily work of repentance in our lives.

One scriptural metaphor to describe this process is that we "put off" our old ways of relating and "put on" the new ways of relating, sometimes referred to as "the mind of Christ." Some primary references giving more detail on this are Romans 13:12–14, Ephesians 4:22–25, Colossians 3:8–14, and 1 Thessalonians 5:8. This metaphor indicates a need for awareness, intentionality, focus, and consistency.

PUTTING IT ALL TOGETHER:
HOW REPENTANCE WORKS IN DAILY LIFE

When Jesus told people to repent, and when Peter told the crowd to repent in Acts 2, they called people to embrace a new trajectory in life—the trajectory of following Jesus.

The initial act of committing our lives to becoming followers of Jesus is a game changer. *But it is just the beginning.* Living a lifestyle of repentance is the bedrock of apprenticing with Jesus and embracing the transformation he came to make available to us. It is a lifestyle... not a "one-off" decision.

Repentance is a difficult orientation to consistently engage for two primary reasons:

- The culture we live in is a culture of entitlement and victimhood. It is a blame game designed to allow us to avoid responsibility, which is the opposite of repentance.

- We often confuse repentance with self-judgment and self-contempt. These reject God's grace and mercy (Romans 11:31–32), preferring condemnation and focus on self. By contrast, repentance directs our attention to others. It softens our hearts toward others and leads us to work to repair the damage done, seek forgiveness, and go again. It inspires us to want to do better.

A LIFESTYLE OF REPENTANCE LEADS TO A LIFESTYLE OF LOVE

A lifestyle of repentance is an ongoing way of embracing humility and exhibiting care for others. Even when you feel someone is entirely unreasonable, have plenty of their own stuff going on, are primarily to blame, or are not recognizing all the great efforts you have put forth thus far in your relationships, repentance focuses on the impact *you* are generating. The results you have are the richest source of clarity regarding your impact, not your good intentions and efforts.

A lifestyle of repentance puts you on the path to transforming your expression of love with others and embracing God's love for you in a more intimate, visceral, freeing, joyous way.

DIRECTLY APPLYING THIS NOW

As part of your vision for this journey, you have identified key relationships and situations you desire to engage. Consider the discipline of repentance in relation to the specifics of your vision. Consider your impact on others and yourself in those specific situations.

Where have you missed the mark? Have you acknowledged that? Have you acknowledged it to those harmed? Missing the mark can be something simple, like being indifferent in the moment, not listening, blaming the other; or it might be something more dramatic. Have you resorted to avoidance, minimizing, dismissing, shame, or self-judgment? Have you allowed yourself to get in touch with the emotional impact on those affected?

All I am asking you to do is to start considering these things. We are talking about the work of a lifetime. The need for the discipline of repentance never goes away. It is the path of connection, growth, awareness, joy, sweet sorrow, acceptance, and surrender.

LOOKING AHEAD...

It is amazing to me that at the very beginning of this journey, Jesus tells us to embrace the orientation that encompasses all other instructions that follow. The Sermon on the Mount, the Beatitudes, the entirety of his instruction in the Gospels, and its further unfolding in the rest of the New Testament—all of this is wrapped up in the initial request he made, that we repent. Everything that follows helps us stay the course of that new trajectory and commitment to change, and to renew the commitment when we lose our way.

TOPIC: CHARTING A NEW TRAJECTORY

Look at what you wrote after the last chapter for your vision statement. Think about the areas of your life where you need to change the trajectory (repentance) in order to move forward. Journal regarding that and, if needed, clarify what you have written thus far for your vision statement so it is as actionable as possible.

VISION FOCUS:

If you have not started yet on a vision statement, you can review the parts of Chapter 1 that discuss that and start on your vision statement now.

Name at least one important relationship you are considering engaging as a part of your vision for this *Apprenticing Jesus* study. If you have more than one relationship that you desire to improve and create newness in, write them all down for now. You can hone it down in the coming weeks.

_____

Name at least one important area of your life that you are interested in changing, growing in, or overcoming obstacles in.

_____

As you pray and as you go through your day, consider these areas and ask God to reveal to you other areas of importance that you may not be considering. Be open to gaining clarity regarding what you are willing to commit to accomplish in your life over the next eight weeks.

DAILY SCRIPTURE
Jeremiah 29:11: "I know what I'm doing. I have it all planned out—plans to take care of you, not abandon you, plans to give you the future you hope for."

CHAPTER 3

JESUS AND THE PRACTICE OF SILENCE AND SOLITUDE

Jesus's commitment to the spiritual disciplines of solitude, silence, and prayer was remarkable. I have always marveled at it. He was the perfect man, with no sin. He was the expression of God in the flesh. Yet, even he felt the need to spend significant amounts of time in prayer with his heavenly father, often staying up all night.

Often Jesus prayed by himself (Matthew 14:23; Mark 1:35, 6:46–47; Luke 5:16). Sometimes he took a few key disciples with him (Mark 9:2, Luke 9:18). He would remove himself from the hustle and bustle of his life and seek solitude and silence for prayer. He also was explicit in his instructions to his disciples on how to pray.

The spiritual disciplines of silence, solitude, and contemplative prayer (a silent attentiveness to God's grace—his divine, unmerited favor) are foundational to shifting the posture of our hearts from reactivity, defensiveness, and avoidance to love, courage, patience, kindness, empathy, and compassion. They also are fundamental practices that support living a lifestyle of repentance.

We will be exploring the depths of prayer throughout this study. We will begin by focusing on the foundational place of solitude and stillness.

GOD'S FIRST LANGUAGE

> Earth was a soup of nothingness, a bottomless emptiness, an inky blackness. God's Spirit brooded like a bird above the watery abyss. (Genesis 1:2, MSG)
>
> The earth was without form and an empty waste, and darkness was upon the face of the very great deep. The Spirit of God was moving (hovering, brooding) over the face of the waters. (Genesis 1:2, AMP)

Consider that God's first language—as he hovered and brooded over the inky blackness—was silence. Silence was his way of being before he spoke and created light (Genesis 1:3). I am not trying to

33

make some sort of theological statement here. I am asking you to simply consider that silence is a significant part of God's communication with man—at least "silence" within the contextual understanding of the modern world.

Consider that it is in silence that we can once again establish a deep connection to God as we clear our minds of the chatter of the world and become renewed and aware of God's presence within us and around us. Silence is an essential element of practicing stillness (Psalm 46:10).

Silence sets the foundation. In the beginning was God. And Genesis 1 says he created the heavens and the earth, which were without form, empty and dark.

And then, in Genesis 1:3, a marvelous thing occurred—God spoke. With language, he created light and brought order to the heavens and earth he had created.

SILENCE AND SOLITUDE: MAKING ROOM FOR GOD

The spiritual disciplines, as Christians have understood and practiced them for centuries, are disciplines designed to help us be active and effective in the spiritual realm of our own hearts, now spiritually alive by grace, in relation to God and his kingdom. They are designed to help us withdraw from total dependence on the merely human or natural and to depend also on the ultimate reality, which is God and his kingdom.[7]

This week, consider the power of solitude and silence to make room for God in your life. Solitude and silence are spiritual disciplines of abstinence—abstinence from human contact, including human-generated noise and activity, as well as absence from dependence on thought.

Henri Nouwen calls solitude the "furnace of transformation."[8] He writes:

For us, solitude most often means privacy. We have come to the dubious conviction that we all have a right to privacy. Solitude thus becomes like a spiritual property for which we can compete on the free market of spiritual goods. But there is more. We also think of solitude as a station where we can recharge our batteries or as the corner of the boxing ring where our wounds are oiled, our muscles massaged, and our courage restored by fitting slogans. In short, we think of solitude as a place where we gather new strength to continue the ongoing competition in life.

But that is not the solitude of St. John the Baptist, of St. Anthony or St. Benedict, of Charles de Foucauld or the brothers of Taize. For them solitude is not a private therapeutic place. Rather, it is the place of conversion, the place where the old self dies and the new self is born, the place where the emergence of the new man and the new woman occurs.

How can we gain a clearer understanding of this transforming solitude? Let me try to describe in more detail the struggle as well as the encounter that takes place in this solitude.

In solitude I get rid of my scaffolding: no friends to talk with, no telephone calls to make, no meetings to attend, no music to entertain, no books to distract, just me—naked, vulnerable, weak, sinful, deprived, broken—nothing. It is this nothingness that I have to face in my solitude, a nothingness so dreadful that everything in me wants to run to my friends, my work and my distractions so that I can forget my nothingness and make myself believe that I am worth something. But that is not all. As soon as I decide to stay in my solitude, confusing ideas, disturbing images, wild fantasies, and weird associations jump about in my mind like monkeys in a banana tree. Anger and greed begin to show their ugly faces. I give long, hostile speeches to my enemies and dream lustful dreams in which I am wealthy, influential, and very attractive—or poor, ugly, and in need of immediate consolation. Thus I try again to run from the dark abyss of my nothingness and restore my false self in all its vainglory.[9]

SOLITUDE, REALITY, AND THE PATH TO TRANSFORMATION

What Nouwen so beautifully describes is the lifestyle of repentance, in particular, the conversion process in the context of the spiritual disciplines. We have considered briefly the power of our minds and hearts to self-deceive, thus clouding our ability to accurately see our current reality. This is never completely going away. It is therefore beneficial to increase awareness of the strategies you depend on to navigate life. To make the transition to true reality requires full trust and confidence in God to be with you each step of the way, no matter how perilous it seems. This puts you on the path toward transforming your character from its automatic default of selfishness to reflecting the goodness of God.

Solitude is a practice that, over time, enables an awareness of these selfish strategies to bubble up out of your unconscious. Once you are aware of a thought pattern that erodes goodness, you can do something about it.

To begin, "sit with" the limiting thought pattern rather than resist it. Be curious about your motives driving it and relax into it, allowing God to be with you in it rather than resisting, denying, and stuffing it away. Ultimately, this will enable you to "put it off" and "put on" a new strategy and way of being (Colossians 3:8–10). You can transform it—meaning you can convert it from limiting to flourishing.

Henri Nouwen once asked Mother Teresa for spiritual direction. "Spend one hour each day in adoration of your Lord, she said, and never do anything you know is wrong. Follow this and you'll be fine." [10]

Spend one hour a day in adoration of your Lord and never do anything you know is wrong, and you will be all right. Solitude gives you a chance to be with God without disruption, to be with yourself without distraction, and to be with Jesus without separation. It is an opportunity to notice your attitudes and heart and consider them without the need to justify, excuse, or defend. It is an opportunity to notice your judgments of yourself and others. You then have a chance to come before God for forgiveness and to bask in his mercy and grace. Solitude is an opportunity to be okay with your brokenness and to seek God to turn the hardened, stony areas of your heart back to flesh. It is an opportunity to be naked before the Lord and to seek his guidance and presence.

Silence and solitude help clear the distractions that keep us from practicing stillness—the precursor to centering on God (Psalm 46:10). They create space for experiencing God.

WHERE SPIRITUAL MINISTRY BEGINS

Solitude is where spiritual ministry begins. It is where Jesus listened to God. It is where we listen to God. Henri Nouwen says:

Sometimes I think of life as a big wagon wheel with many spokes. In the middle is the hub. Often in ministry, it looks like we are running around the rim trying to reach everybody. But God says "Start in the hub; live in the hub. Then you will be connected with all the spokes, and you won't have to run so fast. It is precisely in the hub, in that communion with God, that we discover the call to community. It's remarkable that solitude always calls us to community. In solitude you realize you're part of a human family and that you want to lift something together."

Why is solitude so important? It is your opportunity to listen to and to converse with the One who calls you beloved. To pray is to let that voice speak to the center of your being, to your guts, and to resound in your whole being. No matter how many times or how far you have missed the mark, he still calls you his beloved. He actually uses your sin and your passions for his good—even though you misuse them. They can become the path through which he redeems and transforms you. To take time for those redemptive conversations is to embrace God's love for you. And these conversations can be had with words or without words.

Whatever other voices you listen to about what you are or are not, take time to hear God who calls you his beloved. If you know and confirm consistently how much God loves you by being in solitude with him, then you can embrace truly trusting that he has your back, no matter what—even when everything is going sideways. The rest that Jesus speaks of in Matthew 11 is birthed in this reality.

Jesus often spent the entire night in prayer. That shows that prayer is not something you always quickly feel or hear, or an insight that suddenly comes to you.

God has called us to community. Why is it so important that solitude comes before community? Because if we do not know we are God's beloved, we will always seek approval from others through the false images we project and the things we do to get love and approval from them. This is *the foundation* for breaking up a life based on scarcity-based survival strategies—the things you do to compensate for what you do not believe is possible from God if you were really just you, "naked" before him.

This lifestyle can be expressed in two words: gratitude and compassion. Gratitude is the antidote for resentment and entitlement. They cannot coexist in the same space. Forgiveness is the forerunner to gratitude, and gratitude is the foundation upon which empathy and compassion are built.

Losses, disappointments, and betrayals invite us to live in resentment, resignation, anger, bitterness, and a hardened heart. But Jesus calls us to gratitude. He says those who lose their lives will gain them. He says that to die to self is gain. He embraced suffering, having faith that it would lead to joy. These realities are all a mystery, but they are part of God's economy of community and ministry.

This all starts with solitude. If you know you are beloved, you will be willing to be with God in whatever is happening. You will notice your assumptions, assessments, and judgments. You will be able to give them up to God, clear them, and create room to experience him. In this way, you create a *new space for living with God and others*. If you know that you are loved by God, you can deal with an enormous amount of both success and failure.

LISTENING IN THE PLACE OF SILENCE

Silence completes and intensifies solitude.[11] God most often speaks to us in a gentle whisper (1 Kings 19:11–13). Silence creates a space for God to speak, for him to do his work in us and with us. It creates a rich environment for us to hear and experience what we would not hear and experience when surrounded by noise and activity. It is an interruption to distraction and desperation and invites the possibility of peace and trust.

There are two ways to embrace silence—externally and internally. External silence means being in a physical location without extraneous noise and distraction. It does not necessarily mean that you are in a place with zero external sounds. Being out in nature, and hearing the sounds of nature expressing the joy of God's creation can be a delightful expression of silence.

Internal silence quiets the endless chatter of thought that tends to run in our brains nonstop. This is what I have referred to earlier as practicing stillness. Practicing stillness of your mind can look like focusing on your breath and clearing your thoughts. As you notice your thoughts, turn your attention inward, let go of your thoughts, and notice what is present. It is an awesome preparation of your mind, heart, and body for spiritual awareness, contemplative prayer, and conversing with God.

Enjoy embracing silence and solitude as you taste the rich fruit of God's goodness in your life.

TOPIC 1: LOVE AND HONESTY IN COMMUNITY

Think about the people who are in your church community, or the friend or group of friends you desire to walk this out with. The value you will receive from this journey will be exponentially higher if you walk it with others committed to the same journey.

VISION FOCUS:

Consider the assets and value of those you are walking this journey with or intend to walk it with. What do they bring to the table that will create value for you and others? Consider this and journal regarding everything that comes to mind.

_____

_____

_____

_____

Consider yourself and the value and assets you will be bringing to the others you are walking this journey with. Consider this, and journal regarding everything that comes to mind.

_____

_____

_____

_____

DAILY SCRIPTURE

Matthew 18:19–20: "Again, I tell you that if two of you on earth agree about anything you ask for, it will be done for you by my Father in heaven. For where two or three come together in my name, there am I with them." (BSB)

Proverbs 27:17: "As iron sharpens iron, so one man sharpens another." (BSB)

DAILY PRACTICE: PRACTICING STILLNESS

Psalm 46:10a: *be still, and know that I am God.*

This week, you are going to practice stillness, using breathing as the mechanism to quiet yourself.

Get in a quiet place, with no distractions. You want to also practice the spiritual disciplines of silence and solitude as you practice stillness.

You can practice this sitting, laying down, or walking. Choose whichever supports you being able to focus best. If you are sitting, sit with your back straight and your feet flat on the floor. If you are lying down, lie is a comfortable pose. If you are walking, walk with your head level, back straight and looking ahead.

- Close your eyes (unless you are walking), and start paying attention to your breathing. Deeply inhale, through your nose, all the way deep into your belly. Your stomach should go out as you inhale, and in as you exhale. Exhale through your mouth. Focus on your breath as you inhale and as you exhale.

- Calm your mind and release the constant chatter of your mind by attending to your breathing. See your breath go in and out in your mind's eye. Your mind may not want to calm down. You may have difficulty releasing the need to think thoughts. This is all perfectly normal and no problem at all. The important thing is to simply bring your attention back to your breathing when you do notice your mind wandering.

- The two most important attitudes to practice this with are PATIENCE and NON-JUDGMENT. Practice this always non-judgmentally with patience. To practice non-judgmentally is to be accepting of whatever is. In other words, even if your mind wanders all the time, you do not judge yourself for not doing it well, you simply notice it, and bring your mind back to focusing on your breathing without resisting that this occurred.

- When you are practicing stillness, you are observing with love—not with resistance, judgment, analysis, or labeling—just observation with love and reverence.

- Turn your attention inward and notice your physical sensations and feelings. Just notice them. Do not feel compelled to do anything about them.

- Do this for at least a few minutes per day. In the beginning, two minutes is a win, and twelve minutes is a home run. Ultimately you will want to expand the time you do this. It is a delightful experience to simply be still and PRACTICE stillness. It sets the stage for a deeper experience of God and yourself.

- In future chapters we will build on this discipline of practicing stillness with various forms of prayer. For this now, simply practice stillness.

CHAPTER 4

THE UNHURRIED LIFE: MERGING AND EMERGING

Dallas Willard, the renowned author, theologian, and philosopher, was once mentoring well-known pastor and author John Ortberg. Ortberg recalls an incident with Dallas when he asked his mentor what he needed to do to be spiritually healthy.

There was a long pause. Then Dallas answered, "You must ruthlessly eliminate hurry from your life."

Ortberg said, "Okay, that's a good one. Now what else is there?"

Another long pause. Then Willard said, "There is nothing else."[12]

"Ruthless" means without pity or compassion, merciless. The principle Willard expressed is that we are to give no quarter to hurry in our lives—we should not allow it to take residence in our hearts, in our minds, in our interactions with others, in our prayer lives, or in our souls.

ENGAGING YOUR VISION

Consider the impact busyness and hurry is having in your life. What impact could practicing rest and stillness have on your life and relationships?

I had the privilege of being around Dallas Willard a few times over the last five years or so of his life. I am struck by how thoroughly he embodied his advice regarding the unhurried life. He was a prolific writer, philosophy professor at the University of Southern California, frequent speaker, and mentor to many protégés. He taught multiday seminars every year—yet I never, ever saw him exhibit one scintilla of hurry—ever. He lived the advice he gave to others. In our culture, we equate hurry and busyness with accomplishment and importance, yet he was extraordinarily accomplished without hurry.

Hurry is a great enemy of the spiritual life in our day. It is corrosive and destructive. As Carl Jung wrote, "Hurry is not of the devil. Hurry is the devil."

Modern-day technology is contributing to this hurriedness and distraction in an unprecedented manner. Social media, texting, video games, and instant connection to basically anything on the internet via portable devices are combining to lower attention levels among children and adults to unheard-of levels. Researchers report that teens that spend hours per week playing video games can have attention spans that are measured in seconds rather than minutes or hours.

Ability to focus on the person in front of you is at an all-time low in our culture. People feel compelled to check their phones for messages via e-mail or text every few minutes. Researchers have noted that multitasking, the ability to juggle several tasks simultaneously with adequate focus and attention, is a myth. It turns out that when you divide your attention among several things simultaneously, focus and performance suffer no matter who you are.

This need for constant stimulation, paradoxically, is leading to deeper levels of isolation and loneliness. There have been dozens and dozens of research papers written documenting this in just the past few years. This is generating a lack of attention, low focus, *and an ever-decreasing ability to be present in the present moment and time.* Many experts believe that the increase in isolation and its subsequent decrease in relational connection and intimacy is also accelerating addictive behaviors of all kinds in our culture today.

Another way to put "ruthlessly eliminate hurry" is to "relax"... a deep soul relaxing. I once heard Willard say that Jesus was relaxed in his life. I had never really considered that before.

Today's age is one of distraction, constant frenetic activity, and the drive to go, go, go. This is combined with a culture that compels us to accomplish "necessary" achievement and results. It's easy to fall into the hurry trap.

THE INVITATION TO AN UNHURRIED LIFE

Jesus's invitation to live an unhurried life is clear:

> Are you tired? Worn out? Burned out on religion? Come to me. Get away with me and you'll recover your life. I'll show you how to take a real rest. Walk with me and work with me—watch how

I do it. Learn the unforced rhythms of grace. I won't lay anything heavy or ill-fitting on you. Keep company with me and you'll learn to live freely and lightly. (Matthew 11:28–30, MSG)

Listen to his message again—same verses, this time in the New International Version:

Come to me, all you who are weary and burdened and I will give you rest. Take my yoke upon you and learn from me, for I am gentle and humble in heart, and you will find rest for your souls. For my yoke is easy and my burden is light. (Matthew 11:28–30, NIV)

THE ALTERNATIVE TO APPRENTICESHIP

It seems that to many, the idea of being a disciple of Jesus is a hard and difficult path to take. It most definitely is not the path of least resistance. But consider the cost of non-discipleship also. A life that does not follow Jesus, ultimately, can be a life dictated by our compulsions, fixations, ego, and defense mechanisms—always striving to be our own savior and ultimately failing. Let's keep the cost of discipleship as laid out in Matthew 11 in perspective.

AFTER "REPENT" COMES "BELIEVE AND FOLLOW"

In chapter 2, we discussed the initial invitation of Jesus to all of us to repent. That was the first of three actions he invites us to. First "repent," then "believe," then "follow."

In Mark 1:15 Jesus said, "Repent and believe the good news." To repent includes undergoing a genuine change of heart and mind. It means to change one's mind, purpose, and trajectory. It is a conversion from a contracted, survival-based expression of yourself to an expanded, generous, flourishing expression of yourself.

In Mark 1:14–17, where Jesus invites onlookers to repent, believe, and follow, the word "believe" means to put your confidence into—i.e., to put your confidence into this declared good news.[13]

The good news Jesus asked them to be confident in was the news that the kingdom of God was *at hand.* In other words, the kingdom was available at that very moment in time. It was near, it was surrounding them, it was immediately accessible, not far away or sometime in the distant future. Jesus intended to unfold for them how to access that kingdom and to embrace it, live it, internalize it, manifest its power, and share it with others.

Immediately on the heels of this invitation to repent and believe, he invited potential apprentices to follow him (Mark 1:17). And that invitation stands for us today. Jesus is inviting you to be with him, to accompany him, to learn from his words and actions, to model his way of being, to assist him, and to discipline yourself to be and do what he was and did.

He is inviting you to live your life as he would live it if he were you.

THE EASY YOKE

Jesus's declaration in Matthew 11:28–30 contains tremendous insight into the beginning attitudes that will open the door for a transition from hurriedness to rest. In this passage, Jesus says, "Come to me, all you who are weary and burdened and I will give you rest. Take my yoke upon you and learn from me, for I am gentle and humble in heart, and you will find rest for your souls. For my yoke is easy and my burden is light."

WEARIED AND BURDENED

The word "weary" means to tire one's self with toil and labor.[14] To be burdened is to feel the weight of a burden. Our burden is all the things we think we need to do in order for life to turn out. In Jesus's day, part of that burden was the oppressive list of do's and don'ts that the Pharisees imposed on the followers of their religion. But I don't think the burden of Jesus's hearers was limited to that, nor is it limited to that today. Our burden is the weight of the entire package of everything we think we need to do for life to work. It also is the circumstances we sometimes find ourselves in through no fault of our own.

Jesus's invitation to come to him in Matthew 11:28 is analogous to his invitation to follow him in Mark 1:17. In Matthew, his promise to us, if we come to him, is that he will give us rest. The word "rest" in Matthew 11:28 means to "cause to rest up, cause to cease or desist from."[15] The rest Jesus promises is tied to us ceasing or desisting from the normal patterns of life we think will carry the day for us. It is to relax into *his* provision rather than relating to both your material and spiritual life with an unending need to achieve and accomplish something to have what you think you need.

To actually stop and consider this as a real possibility can be disorienting. In many ways, it doesn't look possible (what else is there besides accomplishment and achievement?). It is difficult to see any clear path forward toward such a release. It is so far outside the norm of our typical way of relating that it is difficult to even conceive of it. But I am asking you to be open to the yoke Jesus promises and consider it, over time. As you do, think about the rationale Jesus gives for encouraging us to take this on.

IN A WORD—REST

Why take on Jesus's yoke? The most obvious answer is that you will receive rest. Not just normal rest—rest for your soul. This is a soul-penetrating rest and relaxation that quenches, revitalizes, and restores. What an invitation in today's world of exhaustion, sleep deprivation, anxiety, tension, distraction and hurriedness! If there were no other reason to follow Jesus as his apprentice, this alone would do it for me.

If you already consider yourself a follower of Jesus, consider this. If you feel consistently weary and burdened, then you are missing something. Jesus's invitation here is part of that something.

Consider the way of being Jesus promises to engage you with: gentleness and humility. It brings tears to my eyes when I consider specific times in my life when someone showed me gentleness of spirit and loving humility during times when I was overwhelmed, wearied, and burdened. It felt like cool water in a parched desert, like fresh oxygen in an oxygen-deprived world. I remember specific times when these qualities felt like a wave of goodness and love washing over me. It felt like a taste of heaven.

Jesus comes to us in gentleness and humility, asking us to simply follow him. And he promises to alleviate the sense of weariness and burden we carry and replace it with a soul-penetrating rest. Here is a breakdown of his invitation to us:

In Matthew 11:28-30, Jesus said, "Take my yoke upon you." Why? Because:

- *I am gentle* (enduring all things with an even temper, tender of spirit, free from haughty self-sufficiency, soothing, assuaging)[16]
- *I am humble* (low place, especially of low rank)[17]
- I am gentle and humble *in heart* (the seat and center of a man's life in which his distinctive character manifests itself)[18]
- *My yoke is easy* (apt for use, useful, good to be done)[19] [20]
- *My burden is light* (easy to bear)[21]

Jesus also told us what would happen to us if we did take up his yoke—he gave a promise.

- *You will learn from me* (to learn by study or observation—to understand)[22]
- *You will find rest for your soul*

As it says in *The Message:*

> Come to me. Get away with me and you'll recover your life. I'll show you how to take a real rest. Walk with me and work with me—watch how I do it. Learn the unforced rhythms of grace. I won't lay anything heavy or ill-fitting on you. Keep company with me and you'll learn to live freely and lightly. (Matthew 11:28-30)

To ruthlessly eliminate hurry is to embrace the possibility of rest for your soul.

ELIMINATING HURRY

I propose that eliminating hurry has more to do with who you are in life—how you show up—than it does with what you do. However, what you do does matter, and how you go about it matters. For example, contemplative spiritual disciplines are something we do. It's pretty difficult to just snap your fingers and become unhurried. But over time, contemplative spiritual disciplines shift the posture of our hearts—how we are relating in life. This is an invitation to an entirely new level of effectiveness in intentional living.

You can practice silence, solitude, stillness, and various forms of prayer we will be covering in future chapters whenever you choose. You do not have to have a relaxed demeanor or to be stress and anxiety free in order to enter into these disciplines. They are key to leading the way to unhurriedness if you choose to engage them intentionally, regularly, with a vision for being present and connected to self, God, and others.

I invite you to experience the impact solitude, silence, and stillness have as you use them to undergird your prayer life. They are the foundation to Awakening Prayer. Awakening Prayer is my phrase for a series of contemplative prayer disciplines that we are going to cover in this study. Thus far, we have covered solitude, silence and practicing stillness. There are more unique prayer disciplines to come…some that are prayer "without words" and some that are prayer with words. I am so excited to share these with you as we work through this study because, as a whole, they have completely, utterly transformed my prayer life. And, I know they can do the exact same thing for you.

The spiritual disciplines, including contemplative prayer disciplines as mentioned in the previous paragraph, create space to start noticing and engaging things you previously did not notice. They are an invitation to get off the treadmill of self-imposed expectations, the tyranny of the urgent, the mindless rush into the day. They both directly and indirectly impact the posture of your heart. They integrate your mind, soul, and spirit. They connect your head to your heart and instinctual drives.

In our western civilization culture, we are all in our head—intellect rules. The contemplative spiritual disciplines connect the head and the heart, mind, body, and soul. They enable you to transcend just considering all these things cognitively…in your head. The issues of our lives reside in our hearts (Proverbs 4:23), and the results of these issues take root in our bodies and emotions. The spiritual disciplines move you toward deeper levels of awareness of what truly is happening in your heart, body, and mind. They help create new awareness.

As an apprentice of Jesus, your life is not about you. You are about life—the life you have been invited into—the kingdom-of-heaven life. *Embracing the spiritual disciplines helps enable you to rest and relax into the calling God has for you.* You can rest into the knowledge that God's Spirit weaves your participation as a single thread within a life-renewing pattern. This helps connect you to the source of life within God's transformative community of love.

The following verses beautifully describe this:

> Just as a body, though one, has many parts, but all its many parts form one body, so it is with Christ. For we were all baptized by one Spirit so as to form one body—whether Jews or Gentiles, slave or free—and we were all given the one Spirit to drink. Even so the body is not made up of one part but of many. (1 Corinthians 12: 12–14, NIV)

> For by the grace given me I say to every one of you: Do not think of yourself more highly than you ought, but rather think of yourself with sober judgment, in accordance with the faith God has distributed to each of you. For just as each of us has one body with many members, and these members do not all have the same function, so in Christ we, though many, form one body, and each member belongs to all the others. (Romans 12:3–6, NIV)

> Through these he has given us his very great and precious promises, so that through them you may participate in the divine nature, having escaped the corruption in the world caused by evil desires. (2 Peter 1:4, NIV)

Your life is not about you. You are about life. And that life is about merging and emerging.

MERGING AND EMERGING

Jesus repeatedly said the kingdom of heaven was at hand—presently available—and spent much of his three-year ministry teaching others how to live in and manifest that kingdom. Consider that each of us has a "kingdom." You have a kingdom and I have a kingdom. *Our kingdom is that which we have authority over.* It is the sphere of influence of our

50

life and all that entails. We each choose how to "rule" our kingdom on a moment-by-moment basis every day.

God has a kingdom also, and Jesus said he came to unveil the accessibility of that kingdom in a new and pronounced way to all who would hear. He repeatedly talked about the nature of his kingdom, and he invited his listeners to merge with it and subordinate their kingdom to his kingdom—working together, being mentored by him in that relationship.

Please allow me to give an analogy. Let's say you are a carpenter. I owned a construction company for over a decade and I was always so impressed with my finish carpenters.

I, as the owner of the company, was blown away with the skill level of most of my finish carpenters. Finish carpenters, in many ways, are artists. Their skills are at the top of their profession.

Jesus, interestingly, was a carpenter. He lived it. In the construction trades in today's world, people learn to become expert carpenters through apprenticeship. They literally apprentice themselves to a master carpenter who, day by day, moment by moment, works alongside the novice, teaching them how to do finish carpentry by doing and teaching. They are actually doing it together, and the apprentice learns the nuances of that trade (of which there are thousands) as they try it out and either screw it up or get it done correctly. When they screw it up, their master carpenter who is teaching them actually shows them how to correctly do it by showing them.

This is what apprenticeship is all about. Learning by doing and being subsequently instructed by a master. This is exactly what Jesus invites us into. We work on living the life he has invited us into, and then he teaches us and instructs us…through his life, as illustrated in the Gospels, through his guidance to us through the Holy Spirit who is here to comfort us as a result of his life, death, resurrection , and ascension into heaven…all of which preceded the coming of the Holy Spirit on the day of Pentecost, and also by his guidance, as Jesus the Christ.

What an amazing journey we have been called to and how amazing that we are actively tutored by God Himself through his expression, as Jesus Christ. This is our calling.

When Jesus declared this available, around 2,000 years ago, most of his followers mistook what it meant to "rule" for some sort of political and social system control. But that was not the kingdom Jesus was referring to when he talked about the kingdom of heaven.

God's invitation through Jesus is to take your kingdom—your rule over your sphere of influence in your life—and to put it under the rule of Jesus Christ. This rule is the kingdom of heaven or God's kingdom. That is the essence of the invitation. If you do this, then the kingdom of heaven goes wherever you go. Wherever you go, it is present in a palpable sense if you are living by its principles, disciplines, and practices. This means you live your life by kingdom-of-heaven attitudes, actions, and ways of being rather than your former attitudes, actions, and ways of being.

To commit to merging yourself with God's kingdom integrates you into God's community of transformative love, the body of Christ. You become a critical part of establishing the kingdom of God for eternity. The establishment of God's kingdom is happening right now with his sons and daughters who are on board, and it will continue eternally.

Living in the kingdom of God is much more than acting on Romans 10:9—confessing Jesus as Lord and believing God raised him from the dead—and then living any way you want for the rest of your life, waiting for your physical death before you can enter the heavenly realm. That is a completely contrary view of the life Jesus is inviting us into as his apprentices.

Instead, the big game we are invited to is to transform our character by embracing and developing the heart of goodness Jesus unveils. Rather than being preoccupied with fear, unworthiness, guilt, frustration, and "failing to do the right thing," allow yourself to be drawn into and immersed in the delight of being a part of an all-encompassing plan that is already in place. Rather than being consumed with your "woundedness" or "brokenness" or "fall from grace" or "inescapable sin nature," how about recognizing the all-encompassing invitation extended to you to embrace God's kingdom, merge your kingdom with his, and start living in the intentionality and freedom that its grace, mercy, forgiveness, and redemption offer?

The apostle Paul beautifully expresses this invitation in his epistle to the Ephesians:

> For this reason I kneel before the Father, from whom every family in heaven and on earth derives its name. I pray that out of his glorious riches he may strengthen you with power through his Spirit in your inner being, so that Christ may dwell in your hearts through faith. And I pray that you, being rooted and established in love, may have power, together with all the Lord's holy people, to grasp how wide and long and high and deep is the love of Christ, and to know this love that surpasses knowledge—that you may be filled to the measure of all the fullness of God. Now to him who is able to do immeasurably more than all we ask or imagine, according to his power that is at work within us, to him be glory in the church and in Christ Jesus throughout all generations, for ever and ever! Amen. (Ephesians 3:14–20, NIV)

This kingdom orientation, this merging of our lives with his, strengthens us in authenticity, vulnerability, openness, freedom, and courage. It allows us to stand naked before God rather than cover ourselves in shame as Adam did in the garden as he blamed both God and Eve for his actions. Rather than getting caught in avoiding, hiding, blaming, or shaming, an apprentice of Jesus is invited to embrace a personal place in the kingdom of heaven *now*, and to adopt *that* way of being, which brings freedom, intimacy, trust, optimism, connection, and courage. It is a life of faith, hope, and love rather than control, cynicism, and self-protection.

Living as an apprentice of Jesus includes merging your kingdom with Jesus's kingdom of heaven. It also includes merging yourself into the oneness of the body of Christ. There is a deep rest in that—a connection that destroys isolation and self-sufficiency, replacing it with oneness and unity with God and his family.

And this merging results in an emerging:

- Emerging into the true essence of who you (specifically you) are created to be for the world.

- Emerging from all the survival strategies you employ to be your own savior rather than embracing Jesus as your savior.

- Emerging from resistance into acceptance and surrender, acceptance of your current reality as God's redemptive provision and path forward for you.

APPRENTICING WITH JESUS THROUGH PRAYER: RELAXING IN GOD'S GOODNESS

Once you see that you do not have to "carry the whole load," you can practice relaxing in God's goodness—in other words, to practice the spiritual discipline of stillness.

Psalm 46:10 says, "Be still and know that I am God." One translation of the word "still" in that verse means to "cease your efforts." It is interesting that ceasing and desisting are also connected to embracing the soul-rest Jesus references in Matthew 11.

The word for "know" in this verse is fascinating. It is the Hebrew word *yada*. The comedian Jerry Seinfeld made this Hebrew word famous with his "yada, yada, yada" invocation. The closest synonyms to its usage in the Old Testament are "to discern" and "to recognize."[23] Baker's Evangelical Dictionary states that *yada* is "to apprehend and experience reality. Knowledge is not the possession of information, but rather, its exercise or actualization."

While *yada* is frequently translated "to know," its meaning is in fact far broader. The meaning includes considered knowledge, learning, contemplation, and ability to distinguish, to possess a developed sense of awareness, heightened consciousness, perceptions, intuition, and discernment. The physical expression of these may include declaration and acknowledgement, performance, creativity, and skilled use of the five physical senses. When the Scripture says, "Adam knew Eve," the word "knew" is *yada*.

To sum it up, yada is the developed expression of an intimate knowledge of God, incorporating every aspect of our lives as an act of worship.

Yada has been described as an abbreviation for the entirety of Yahweh's message to mankind.

It is not referring to an intellectual or cognitive knowing alone. It has to do with knowing through the mind, heart, body, and soul, including the five physical senses.

It makes perfect sense that we would have to cease all activity and be still in order to even have a shot at this level of experiential knowing.

Two of the primary spiritual disciplines we have discussed that support this are solitude and silence. They set the stage for stillness and prayer becoming transformational rather than transactional. *Transactional* means to do something to produce a particular result in an expected time frame. I think that is how many approach prayer. *Transformational* indicates a leap of faith into the unknown—perhaps having a sense of what it will look like but being aware that the way it actually happens will be outside the realm of your anticipated expectations. Transformational leads to "brand new." And, when something is brand new, it almost always is different than what we thought it would be. "New" is beyond our historically established expectations. It goes beyond our assumptions of "the way it is" as well as our assumptions of "the way it needs to be." It is an adventure, and the way God designed it, it is an adventure that is embodied...an experience that includes our head, our heart and our body.

THE SPIRITUAL DISCIPLINES AS THE FOUNDATION OF COMMUNITY

Silence and solitude are disciplines by which we create some space in which God can act. They create space for something to happen that we hadn't planned for or counted on. As mentioned previously, Jesus often spent time in solitude—in a solitary place—sometimes for an entire night. He would spend time in solitude with God, *then* gather his apostles—forming community—and *then*, and *only* then, go out and minister. So often we get the ministry of Jesus backwards. We start out in ministry or activity to generate results ourselves; then if that doesn't work, we go to community—working to get others to pitch in and help—and then, if all else fails, we go to prayer.

Solitude is being with God and God alone. It is the foundation of where you find the rest Jesus promises.

You might have noticed that when you try to practice silence and stillness, your mind starts jumping to your to-do list and other matters. It is not easy to sit and trust that in solitude, God will speak to you—not as a magical voice, but that in some way he will let you know something gradually over the years. And in that word from God you will find the inner peace from which to live your life.

A simple way to quiet your heart and mind to practice stillness can include the following:

- Get in a quiet place with no distractions (silence and solitude)

- I usually also close my eyes to prevent distraction.

- If you are sitting, sit upright with your feet on the floor. If you are lying down, then lie down in a comfortable position.

- Breathe deeply, inhaling through your nose and exhaling through your mouth. Your stomach should go out as you inhale and come in as you exhale.

- Use the mechanism of "attending to" your breathing (focusing and paying attention to your breathing) to help you clear your mind of extraneous thought.

- Quiet your mind as you attend to your breathing.

- When your mind wanders and you notice it, gently bring your attention back to your breathing.

- Enjoy simply being, without any need to think or do.

- Notice your internal physical sensations, emotions, and feelings. If you don't notice anything, then notice that. Do this non-judgmentally. Be patient. However you do it is fine.

- Do this for several minutes until your mind is settling down and not whirling, and you can start simply being in the awareness of your body's internal state.

This is practicing stillness. And, it sets the stage for the contemplative discipline of practicing the presence of God—consciously being in his presence. We will focus on that soon enough. For now, I am going to ask you to simply practice stillness in silence and solitude. Don't worry if you find it difficult to quiet your mind and clear your tendency to constantly think of things. That is normal. Simply practicing focusing on your breathing and clearing extraneous thoughts, and turning your attention to your inner self and noticing your physical sensations and feelings is enough for now.

This practice sets the stage for Jesus's invitation to ring true.

I imagine him saying, "Come to me. Get away with me and you'll recover your life. I'll show you how to take a real rest. Walk with me and work with me—watch how I do it. Learn the unforced rhythms of grace. I won't lay anything heavy or ill-fitting on you. Keep company with me and you'll learn to live freely and lightly."

TRUST: THE FOUNDATIONAL MINDSET OF PRAYER

Trust in the Lord with all your heart and lean not on your own understanding; in all your ways submit to him, and he will make your paths straight. (Proverbs 3:4–6, NIV)

Author Thomas Keating states:

The Christian spiritual path is based on a deepening trust in God. It is trust that first allows us to take that initial leap in the dark, to encounter God at deeper levels of ourselves. And it is trust that guides the intimate refashioning of our being, the transformation of our pain, woundedness, and unconscious motivation into the person that God intended us to be.

Because trust is so important, our spiritual journey may be blocked if we carry negative attitudes toward God from early childhood. If we are afraid of God or see God as an angry father-figure, a suspicious policeman, or a harsh judge, it will be hard to develop enthusiasm, or even an interest, in the journey.[24]

It is trust that, more than anything else, allows us to rest in the presence of God and be transformed by his love and grace in the journey of apprenticeship. During the Sermon on the Mount Jesus said:

> Which of you, if your son asks for bread, will give him a stone? Or if he asks for a fish, will give him a snake? If you, then, though you are evil, know how to give good gifts to your children, how much more will your Father in heaven give good gifts to those who ask him! (Matthew 7:9–11, NIV)

In Luke, he again instructed his disciples:

> Which of you fathers, if your son asks for a fish, will give him a snake instead? Or if he asks for an egg, will give him a scorpion? If you then, though you are evil, know how to give good gifts to your children, how much more will your Father in heaven give the Holy Spirit to those who ask him! (Luke 11:11-13, NIV)

Jesus is directly addressing the issue of trusting in God's goodness toward you, specifically and individually. Can we trust him to be with us in every situation? Jesus's answer is a resounding "YES!"

Trust is closely related to belief and faith. In 1 Corinthians 13:7, the word translated "believes" ("love believes") is also translated "trust" in some versions ("love trusts"). Who does love trust? First and foremost, it trusts God and his goodness and commitment to always have our backs as we live eternally in his kingdom as his disciples. Trust, faith, belief, and love: these are deeply connected and intertwined realities that make a huge difference in the quality of our lives on a day-to-day basis.

TRUST, LOVE, FAITH, AND HOPE

To truly love another is a risky, vulnerable act. Faith believes that God will see us through the ultimate disappointments and suffering that result from trusting and loving imperfect people—and we are all imperfect. Trust believes he will redeem the losses, disappointments, and betrayals.

58

A hallmark of great relationships is open and candid conversation, not withholding or avoiding. This requires courage, acting in the face of fear. The fear we face in relationship is embedded in the vulnerability of possible rejection, abandonment, or failure. Love requires trusting God in the face of that vulnerability. Trust is a leap of faith.

Hebrews 11:1 says faith is the "substance of things hoped for, the evidence of things not seen." To trust as an act of faith is to embrace hope—to step into the unknown for the possibility of something that currently is not seen.

In that gap of the unknown—that possible abyss—God meets us and completes love in connection with another. Or he stays with us when we fail. He promises us he will be with us no matter what, which gives us the courage and fortitude to go again.

In the next chapter, we will dive deeper into this intimate connection with God, and how we can grow this connection of intimacy with our God.

ABIDING AND RESTING

In addition to the practices of stillness in silence and solitude, we will now practice ABIDING AND RESTING.

Be still, and know that I am God. (Psalm 46:10a, NIV)

Come to me, all you who are weary and burdened and I will give you rest. Take my yoke upon you and learn from me, for I am gentle and humble in heart, and you will find rest for your souls. For my yoke is easy and my burden is light. (Matthew 11:28–30, NIV)

PRACTICING STILLNESS

Begin practicing stillness by using breathing as the mechanism to quiet yourself. Every time you practice these contemplative disciplines, start with stillness. It is an amazingly restful practice in and of itself. It also quiets the mind to prepare it for *contemplating God's presence and resting and abiding in his presence.*

After practicing stillness, I have three different resting practices you can engage to practice resting in God. Before trying the resting practices, here are a few tips to help you become still:

Get in a quiet place, with no distractions. You want to also practice the spiritual disciplines of silence and solitude as you engage practicing stillness.

You can practice this sitting, laying down, or walking. Your choice... whatever supports you being able to focus best. If you are sitting, sit with your back straight and your feet flat on the floor. If you are lying down, lie is a comfortable pose. If you are walking, walk with your head level, back straight, and looking ahead.

- Close your eyes (unless you are walking), and start paying attention to your breathing. Deeply inhale, through your nose, all the way deep into your belly. Your stomach should go out as you inhale. Exhale through your mouth. Focus on your breath as you inhale and as you exhale.

- Calm your mind and release the constant chatter of your mind by attending to your breathing. See your breath go in and out in your mind's eye. Your mind may not want to calm down. You may have difficulty releasing the need to think thoughts. This is all perfectly normal and no problem at all. The important thing is to simply bring your attention back to your breathing when you do notice your mind wandering.

- The two most important attitudes to practice this with are PATIENCE and NON-JUDGMENT. To practice non-judgmentally is to be accepting of whatever is. In other words, even if your mind wanders all the time, you do not judge yourself for not doing it well. You simply notice it and bring your mind back without resisting that this occurred.

- When you are practicing stillness, you are observing with love—not with resistance, judgment, analysis, or labeling—just observation with love and reverence.

- Turn your attention inward and notice your physical sensations and feelings. Just notice them. Do not feel compelled to do anything about them.

- Do this for at least a few minutes per day. In the beginning, two minutes is a win, and twelve minutes is a home run. Ultimately you will want to expand the time you do this. It is a delightful experience to simply be still and PRACTICE stillness. It sets the stage for a deeper experience of God and yourself.

- In future weeks we will build on this discipline of practicing stillness with various forms of prayer. But, for now, simply practice stillness.

Now, in addition to practicing stillness, you can practice RESTING in God. Feel free to envision this as resting in Jesus the Son, resting in Christ the Messiah, or resting in God the father, or resting in the bosom of the Holy Spirit. You can try resting in each of these different expressions of God, or focus on the one that you resonate most with. Your choice.
Here are three different suggestions for resting in God's arms.

RESTING PRACTICE NUMBER 1:
RELEASING STRESS AND TENSION

After practicing stillness to quiet your mind and to become mindfully present, notice where you are holding tension or stress in your body. Simply be present with the tension or stress. Do not resist it...don't think of tension or stress as a problem. Don't tell yourself that they shouldn't be there or feel an immediate need to alleviate them. Simply notice how you feel and allow God to be with you.

Then, as you continue to breathe deeply and attend to your breathing, do the following:

- Inhale God's rest and peace deep into your body. Envision it permeating every cell in your body.

- Exhale out all the tension and stress you notice. Just release it into God's mercy and grace.

- Continue this for however much time you have. Don't worry about whether it "is working" or not. Simply try it and enjoy practicing the presence of God—within you and all around you—bathing in his love and peace.

RESTING PRACTICE NUMBER 2:
NOTICING YOUR EMOTIONAL STATE

After practicing stillness to quiet your mind and becoming mindfully present, *notice whatever emotions and feelings you are carrying in your heart and body.* Simply be present with whatever you notice. If you don't notice any emotions or feelings, notice that and be with that. Do not resist whatever you notice…treating it as a problem or trying to alleviate it. Simply notice it and allow God to be with you in it.

Then, as you continue to breathe deeply and attend to your breathing:

- Inhale God's total love and absolute delight for you into your body. Envision it permeating every cell in your body.

- Exhale your love and delight for God. Breathe it out to him. All the while you are staying present in whatever you are feeling emotionally. You might be sad, afraid, ashamed, joyful, or something else. Simply be with whatever it is, accepting it in the present moment, and embody and express through your breath life your love for God and his love for you.

- Continue this for however much time you have to practice it. Don't worry about whether it "is working" or not. Simply practice it and enjoy practicing the presence of God—within you and all around you—bathing you in his love and peace.

RESTING PRACTICE NUMBER 3:
NOTICING MENTAL CHATTER AND/OR ANXIETY AND
EMBRACING AND EXPRESSING DELIGHT WITH GOD

While you are practicing stillness, you will notice that your mind wanders from time to time. Sometimes it persistently wanders and it seems it won't settle down. If you experience this, it is no problem at all. It is fine. Simply notice it and allow God to be with you in it, as you release the thoughts when you notice them and return your attention to your breathing.

During the times when your mental chatter is especially loud, consider what emotion or bodily sensation may be associated with your mind jumping all over the place. Sometimes you will notice some level of anxiety. Sometimes you will not notice anything.

In that moment, though, you can ask God to settle your heart and mind, and practice receiving his peace so that it permeates every cell in your body. Simply practice that with your breathing.

As you continue to breathe deeply and attend to your breathing:

- Inhale God's peace and calm into your body. Envision it permeating every cell in your body.

- Exhale your trust in God as an offering to him. Breathe it out to him. All the while you are staying present in whatever you are feeling. Simply be with whatever it is, accepting it in the present moment, and embody and express through your breath life your trust in God and his goodness towards you.

- Continue this for however much time you have to practice it. Don't worry about whether it "is working" or not. Simply practice it and enjoy practicing trusting God—within you and all around you—bathing you in his calm and peace.

CHAPTER 5

COMMUNING WITH GOD

A great foundation sets up the possibility of building a great house. If the foundation is lousy, it won't matter how well the house is built—it will eventually be compromised and give rise to problems.

The previous chapters have emphasized the spiritual disciplines of silence, solitude, and stillness. These spiritual practices are the foundation of creating deeper connection with God as well as deeper connection to yourself. They calm the soul and help us notice what we are unaware of. They connect our minds with both our hearts and the embodied Christ within. They are the foundational disciplines in creating a deeper relationship with God and with Jesus Christ.

Today, we shift our focus to what Jesus specifically says about prayer. He was as explicitly clear in his comments about prayer as with any topic he discussed during his ministry on earth.

ENGAGING YOUR VISION

Consider the nature and condition of your prayer life. Where do you desire more intimacy in your walk with God? How would that impact the areas in your life where you are currently struggling?

Let's look at this through the lens of Jesus's instructions to his apprentices in the Gospels. We are also his apprentices, with access to his teachings and his heart.

Consider these instructions as if he were here with you, at the kitchen table, visiting. You ask him, "How do we pray?" He says, "I'm glad you asked that! Great question. Here is the answer..."

In the Gospels, Jesus rarely gave a straightforward answer to a question. He almost always answered questions with another question or with a parable—which would provoke an extended series of open considerations. However, Jesus immediately gave explicitly clear answers to at least two questions asked of him.

One was the question regarding the greatest commandment. He immediately said it is to love God with all your heart, soul, mind, and strength, and love your neighbor as yourself (Matthew 22:36–40, Luke 10:25–28). No ambiguity regarding what he meant in that answer!

The second was asked by the disciples as to how they should pray (Luke 11:1–11). An apprentice requested, "Lord, teach us how to pray." And Jesus immediately dove into it. Essentially, he responded, "Okay, this is exactly how you do this—listen up." Jesus also included explicit instruction regarding prayer in the Sermon on the Mount (Matthew 6:5–15). He also explained in depth which attitudes to adopt in prayer.

In the following pages, we are going to look at what Jesus said about prayer and how we can deepen our communion with Jesus Christ as the Master Mentor through God's Spirit.

THE HOUSE OF PRAYER

The spiritual disciplines give us a solid foundation on which to build a "house of prayer" in our own lives, where our daily lives become our place of connection and fellowship with God.

YOUR GO-TO PRAYER PARTNER

Most of us have a go-to "prayer partner" that we pray to—one of the three manifestations of God through the Trinity. Consider whom you normally automatically pray to or relate to most strongly in your prayer life. Is it God the Father? Or is it Jesus Christ? Or is it the gift, the Holy Spirit?

The Trinity is a mystical reality, and its depths are beyond the capacity of the human mind to fully grasp. Nonetheless, I have found that most people have a tendency to pray to just one aspect of the Trinity as their go-to. Take a moment, think about it, and determine yours.

Mine has historically been God the Father. I just automatically pray to him when praying. I am not sure of all the reasons for that, but there are probably many. I always wanted to have a closer relationship and awareness of Jesus Christ in my life, but that seemed a bit far off to me experientially. That connection is growing, however, as I continue to saturate myself in these prayer disciplines.

While I have related to God as a loving, benevolent God of goodness since I was a young child, he still seemed distant to me. He was there, but not viscerally, intimately present—at least not very often. Prayer was something to be done primarily out of duty.

YOUR RELATIONSHIP WITH PRAYER

I'm sure you have your own story about how you have related to God (or not) in prayer throughout your life. Please take time to consider your story and personal experience regarding this. It will be your starting point for where we are going.

Over time, I realized that the way I related to my dad influenced the way I related to God. My parents were divorced when I was six, and after that, I lived with my mom. I saw my dad every few weeks. I knew he loved me, but we just weren't that close. We never really had a relationship with any significant father-son intimacy. By the time I had figured out that I could be proactive as an adult in generating more intimacy with my dad, he had died. I think that dynamic of distance with my earthly father was reflected in my relationship with God, my heavenly father.

Consider how your key relationships early in life may have influenced the way you have related to God. Perhaps previous religious experiences or teachings have also had an influence on how you relate to God. Consider how closely you feel connected to God in prayer. Note where you are on this continuum. Just get a read on your current reality regarding this. *Whether your connection with God is low or high, there is so much more to be had.* Jesus, our Master Mentor, is going to guide us into this realm of deeper connection to him and his Father.

Applying the disciplines and attitudes Jesus taught and modeled has completely revitalized and reoriented my prayer life. The transformation I'm seeing is an ongoing renovation, not an instantaneous change, and it requires consistent engagement, yet it's unmistakably dynamic and real. It is both fascinating and exhilarating to have a sense of deepening connection and progress through practicing and experiencing God's presence. It is worth the effort!

AND THEN, HE SPOKE

As we saw in an earlier chapter, God's first language—as he hovered and brooded over the inky blackness—was silence. Silence was his way of being (Genesis 1:3). Silence is still a significant part of God's communication with man—at least "silence" within the context of the modern world. In silence, we can establish a deep connection with God. Silence sets the foundation.

But then, as recorded in Genesis 1:3, God spoke. God introduced light into the universe through the generative power of language. John 1 chronicles the progression of the power of language that ensued. This is beautifully chronicled in John 1:1–14.

The translation below, done by Greek scholar Clive Scott, might be new to you. It uses the Renaissance scholar Erasmus's translation of the Greek word "logos" in John 1 into the English word "conversation" rather than the more common translation of "logos" into "word" in English. (An endnote below gives more detail on this particular translation.) For me, it brings out marvelous nuance regarding John 1 that deepens my understanding of it and its application. I ask you to consider it. Read it a few times to allow it to sink in.

It all arose out of a Conversation,
a Conversation within God.

In fact, the Conversation was God.

So, God started the discussion, and everything came out of this
and nothing happened without consultation.

This was the life, the life that was the light of men shining in the darkness,
a darkness, which neither understood nor quenched its creativity.

John, a man sent by God, came to remind people
about the nature of the light so that they would observe.

He was not the subject under discussion
but the bearer of an invitation to join in.

The subject of the Conversation, the original light, came into the world,
the world that had arisen out of his willingness to converse.
He fleshed out the words, but the world did not understand.

He came to those who knew the language, but they did not respond.

Those who did became a new creation (his children);
they read the signs and responded.

These children were born out of sharing in the creative activity of God.

They heard the Conversation still going on, here, now, and
took part, discovering a new way of being people.

To be invited to share in a Conversation about the nature of life,
was for them, a glorious opportunity not to be missed.

(John 1:1–14[25])

THE CONVERSATION OF GOD

Let's unpack this passage a bit more. Please consider these words again:

These children were born out of sharing in the creative activity of God.

They heard the Conversation still going on, here, now, and
took part, discovering a new way of being people.

To be invited to share in a Conversation
about the nature of life, was for them, a glorious
opportunity not to be missed.

God has invited us to share in a conversation about the nature of life, which, for us, is a glorious opportunity not to be missed. Jesus is a manifestation of that conversation. His unfolding of the kingdom of heaven—the creative activity of God—birthed children who were born out of sharing in that conversation. That is you and me, if we are committed to be his disciples—his apprentices. You might say we are the children of The Conversation That Is God. You could say it's all about living the conversation, being the conversation, embodying the conversation, embracing and engaging the conversation.

Think about one of the best personal relationships you have now or previously in your life. Odds are it included great conversations. It didn't just include surface conversations about the weather or sports or current events, but meaningful conversation.

German philosopher Martin Heidegger said, "Language is the house of being. In its home, man dwells. Those who think and those who create with words are the guardians of this home."[26]

Author Marciano Guerrero wrote regarding Heidegger's comments:

After years of pondering whatever Martin Heidegger meant by "Language is the House of Being," it finally dawned on me (as I watched the news on TV) that Heidegger meant language is not only a construct, a shelter, an edifice, an abode, but the soul of humanity.

Through language we search heaven and earth; through language we accept or reject God; through language we accept or reject the absolutes that guide the human race ...

We think and we feel by using words. Though words are more adept and adequate to thinking than to feeling, we still recognize that even our deepest emotions must be converted into words to express what we feel. When we immerse ourselves in a good book we feel with and for the characters: with Don Quixote and Sancho we experience the real meaning of friendship; with Anna Karenina and Aschenbach we feel the exquisite pangs of deeply tormented souls; with Remedios The Beauty we ascend to heaven.

Can we build science without language? Isn't language the vessel of patterns, axioms, equations, paradigms, and formulas? Is wisdom achievable without language?

Even the most recalcitrant nihilist or atheist needs language to refute the existence of God; the same God that gave him the gift of language.

When humans master a language, they are never homeless... their spirit, their humanity survives in the House of Being.[27]

70

THE POWER OF LANGUAGE

It is with language that you express your innermost thoughts. It is with language that you express and manifest vulnerability, fear, pride, trust, faith, suffering, joy, love, and hate. Language is the expression of who you are. It translates what is so for you and what is happening to you emotionally and mentally, and it communicates those things for others to consider and engage.

Even unspoken emotional experience is crafted in part by our internal conversations—what we are saying to ourselves internally. It is still about conversation.

Strong, fulfilling, connected relationships tend to be rich in meaningful conversation. Poor, dying relationships tend to be bereft of meaningful conversation and are marked by a withholding of honest, open, authentic communication.

If this is true of our relationships with each other, how different do you think developing a deep, connected relationship with God is? If language and committed conversation are the foundation of great human relationships, wouldn't that be the case with our heavenly Father also?

God wants us to trust him with all that is troubling us—including our frustrations, complaints, despair, and angst. He desires that we express everything—the delights, the appreciations, and the complaints. They are in our hearts anyway. Why not bring them into the light before him?

King David, in the Old Testament, was an amazing example of this. Read the psalms, where he is completely, utterly open in the full range of emotions, concerns, challenges, and delights he was experiencing before God. Scripture says he was a man after God's own heart (Acts 13:22). Surely, God affirmed these expressions of fear, frustration, and angst when describing David's heart.

GOD'S DESIRE FOR US

God's desire from before the foundations of the world was to have a love relationship with you that exceeds anything you've ever considered (Ephesians 1:4–6, 3:20). And that relationship is built upon the foundation of communication and conversation.

God is ready and willing to meet with you. He has done this throughout history. Read Exodus 3:14, 1 Samuel 3:11, 2 Samuel 2:1, Job 40:1, Isaiah 7:3, Jeremiah 1:7, Acts 8:26, and Acts 9:15—an incredible record of God's pursuit of conversation with human beings. He is ready and waiting for us to embrace this unfathomable opportunity to commune with him.

Jesus's instructions in the Gospels are amazingly, explicitly clear regarding how to enjoy this opportunity.

Jesus tells us to ask, seek, knock, wait, request, listen, negotiate, hang in, talk it out, feel God's presence, practice his presence, be in his presence, and bare all before him. That is the dance he invites us into.

Let's close this chapter with Jesus's most explicit instruction on how to pray. I suggest that what follows is the ideal conversational structure for us as apprentices in our prayer life with God.

HOW SHOULD WE PRAY?

Jesus's most extensive and explicitly detailed answer to a question in the Gospels was in response to the question, "How should we pray?"

This is often referred to as the Lord's Prayer. I like to refer to this as The Apprentice's Prayer. He said to pray like this:

Dear Father always near us,
May your name be treasured and loved,

May your rule be completed in us—May your will be done here on earth just
the way it is done in heaven.

Give us today the things we need today,
And forgive us our sins and impositions on you
as we are forgiving all who in any way offend us.

Please don't put us through trials, but deliver us from everything bad.

Because you are the one in charge,
and the glory is all yours—forever—which is just the way we want it!

(Matthew 6:9–13, Dallas Willard Translation)

In your daily practice of prayer, we are going to focus on this magnificent prayer structure laid out by Jesus. It contains the foundation for how to engage God in prayer as apprentices of Jesus.

It is not something to simply be spoken in rote fashion out of religious duty. Quite the contrary, if you are willing to embrace this prayer and make it a part of your life with God, it has the potential to completely revolutionize your prayer life and relationship with God.

This prayer is the heart and soul of a living, breathing, engaged, dynamic, and life-giving daily conversation with God.

This approach to prayer includes three declarations to God and three requests from God—six key orientations to structure your conversational interaction with God. What follows are six contemplation topics for your spiritual practices for the following six days. Each one has a key focus from Jesus's instructions from Matthew 6 for that day. Enjoy.

CONTEMPLATION TOPIC 1:
CLOSENESS AND DELIGHT WITH GOD

DAILY SCRIPTURE

"Dear Father always near us, may your name be treasured and loved." (Matthew 6:9, Dallas Willard Translation—DWT)

Spend time clearing your mind of extraneous thoughts, attending to breathing, calming yourself, becoming "still," being present, and noticing your felt sensations and what you are experiencing.

CONTEMPLATIVE FOCUS

Next, focus on the first aspect of the Apprentice's Prayer, or the Lord's prayer as it is commonly called. We are going to focus on one aspect per day. Ultimately, you can contemplatively pray your way through the entire Lord's prayer in one sitting. But, for now, allow yourself the delicious treat of focusing on only one aspect of the prayer. Simply focus on that one thing as you attend to your breathing. Notice what comes up for you and what occurs to you.

Focus on your first priority—awakening to the loving presence of God in and around you. Declare his name to be treasured and loved and express your adoration of him. Breathe in his delight for you and breathe out your delight in him.

Bathe yourself in this reality. Discard all extraneous thoughts to this contemplation as they occur and bring yourself back to the words of this prayer as you attend to your breathing.

Journal about what you experienced and what you noticed in your quiet time today.

CONTEMPLATION TOPIC 2:
OUR 'JOINT VENTURE' RELATIONSHIP WITH GOD

DAILY SCRIPTURE

"May your rule be completed in us—May your will be done here on earth just the way it is done in heaven." (Matthew 6:10, DWT)

First, spend time clearing your mind of extraneous thought, attending to breathing, calming yourself, becoming "still," being present, and noticing your felt sensations and what you are experiencing.

CONTEMPLATIVE FOCUS

Focus on the next aspect of the Apprentice's Prayer—God's rule being completed in you as you work together with him to do his will here on earth, bringing the kingdom of heaven here.

You could say you are in a joint venture relationship with God. You get to contemplate how you are going to merge "your kingdom" with God's kingdom, today, aligning your will with his kingdom.

Immerse yourself fully in this reality. Discard all extraneous thoughts to this contemplation as they occur and bring yourself back to this only as you attend to your breathing.

Journal about what you experienced and noticed in your quiet time today.

CONTEMPLATION TOPIC 3:
A RELATIONSHIP BUILT ON TRUST

DAILY SCRIPTURE

"Give us today the things we need today." (Matthew 6:11a, DWT)

As always, first spend time clearing your mind of extraneous thought, attending to breathing, calming yourself, becoming "still," being present, and noticing your felt sensations and what you are experiencing.

CONTEMPLATIVE FOCUS

Next, focus on the next aspect of the Apprentice's Prayer—your requests of God for the things you need today.

This can be an amazing aspect of your daily prayer life. Simply contemplate what you have on your plate for today, and contemplate what you may need that you are not thinking of. Then make requests of God relative to the things you need today.

Bathe yourself in this reality. Discard all extraneous thoughts to this contemplation as they occur and bring yourself back to this only as you attend to your breathing.

Another thought to consider: If you have asked for a "need" to be met, and it hasn't been, then perhaps you don't really need it. Or perhaps God's timetable is different than yours. Perhaps it is happening in a way you did not anticipate and thus aren't clearly seeing. God does promise to supply all our needs according to his riches in glory (Philippians 4:19).

Journal about what you experienced and noticed in your quiet time today.

CONTEMPLATION TOPIC 4:
FORGIVENESS, THE FOUNDATION OF GRACE & MERCY

DAILY SCRIPTURE

"And forgive us our sins and impositions on you as we are forgiving of all who in any way offend us." (Matthew 6:12, DWT)

As always, spend time clearing your mind of extraneous thought, attending to breathing, calming yourself, becoming "still," being present, and noticing your felt sensations and what you are experiencing.

CONTEMPLATIVE FOCUS

Next, focus on the next aspect of the Apprentice's Prayer—asking for forgiveness of your sins as you forgive others, clearing all your offenses. This is a life-changing habit if you engage it on a daily basis.

First, consider who in your life you have not forgiven. Forgiveness is not usually a one-off process. You may need to forgive someone a hundred times for something done to you—just forgive them every time it comes up for you.

Second, who are you offended with? Our culture today is overwhelmed with self-righteous offense, across all cultural spectrums. What offenses do you need to clear? Think family, friends, especially enemies, political, cultural, ethnic, regional, national...any offenses in all of these realms. Jesus is asking you to clear those...release them...daily.

After forgiving everyone who comes to mind, and clearing your offenses, consider anything you need to ask God's forgiveness for. List those offenses. Do this all in a quiet, contemplative state.

Immerse yourself fully in this reality. Discard all extraneous thoughts to this contemplation as they occur and bring yourself back to this only as you attend to your breathing.

Journal about what you experienced in your quiet time today, and what you noticed.

CONTEMPLATION TOPIC 5:
OUR REQUEST FOR GOD'S GOODNESS
TO BE MANIFEST TOWARDS US

DAILY SCRIPTURE

"Please don't put us through trials, but deliver us from everything bad. (Matthew 6:13a, DWT)

As always, spend time clearing your mind of extraneous thought, attending to breathing, calming yourself, becoming "still," being present, and noticing your felt sensations and what you are experiencing.

CONTEMPLATIVE FOCUS

Focus on the next aspect of the Apprentice's Prayer—asking God to not put you through trials and to deliver you from everything bad.

At times, I hear Christians say they are "being tested by God" or are "under attack from the devil." Instead of that, try asking God not to put you through trials and to deliver you from everything bad. That is his heart for you.

You can focus on and contemplate God's goodness working its way into your life's details today. After all, he says that is just the way he wants it!

End with contemplating how all glory is due to God and how that is just the way you want it.

Bathe yourself in this reality. Discard all extraneous thoughts as they occur and bring yourself back to this only as you attend to your breathing.

Journal about what you experienced and noticed in your quiet time.

CONTEMPLATION TOPIC 6:
OUR RELATIONSHIP WITH THE PRIME MOVER
FOR ALL OF ETERNITY

DAILY SCRIPTURE

"Because you are the one in charge, and the glory is all yours—forever—which is just the way we want it!" (Matthew 6:13b, DWT)

As always, spend time clearing your mind of extraneous thought, attending to breathing, calming yourself, becoming "still," being present, and noticing your felt sensations and what you are experiencing.

CONTEMPLATIVE FOCUS

Focus on the next aspect of the Apprentice's Prayer, your acknowledgment that God is in charge and deserves all the glory, and you, as an apprentice of Jesus, are very happy with that arrangement! To know that you are a part of his master plan is such a comforting awareness.

Immerse yourself fully in this reality. Discard all extraneous thoughts as they occur and bring yourself back to this only as you attend to your breathing.

Journal about what you experienced in your quiet time, and what you noticed.

CHAPTER 6

THE HEART OF APPRENTICESHIP

"Ultimate Reality is at hand! Change your mind
and believe such good news!"— Mark 1:15[28]

The type of Christianity that apprenticing with Jesus invites us into is a practice-based religion, not a belief or ideology-driven religion. Jesus focused on instructing his disciples how to show up in life—rather than primarily focusing on which ideologies to believe. It was about who they were in their life with others. He realized that what they actually believed would be consistently self-evident in their actions rather than just their words.

Jesus's charge to "repent" is a clear indication of this. As we saw previously, *repent* means to change your mind. That is a lifelong process, not just a one-off decision. To sin means to miss the mark. We often miss the mark. That is why God offers us grace and mercy—the opportunity to go again.

To apprentice with Jesus is a lifetime of growth through changing your heart and mind, awakening to deeper awareness of God, yourself, and others. At times we may wish that making an initial decision would propel us on a straight line toward our new trajectory in life. But to repent is not to ascertain with certainty a new ideology. It is to embark on a completely new way of relating, of being alive. And it is an ebb and flow. It requires change all the time, constant course correction.

The way a sailboat travels upwind is a powerful metaphor for a lifestyle of repentance. It tacks to and fro, zigzagging its way upwind, constantly recalibrating and course correcting to get to the spot it is sailing toward. It is not a perfect straight-line trajectory.

Apprenticing with Jesus is much the same. It is a consistent series of misses, recalibrations, course corrections, and sometimes hitting the mark. This approach to life requires humility, a commitment to awareness, a wakefulness and intentionality. It is not about what you believe intellectually so much as it is about paying attention to how your life is impacting others.

THE HEART OF APPRENTICESHIP

Clearly, to be a disciple includes discipline. It embraces obedience. It involves will and purposefulness. To be an apprentice is to have an interactive relationship with life.

If you were going in for surgery, you would want a surgeon who has done more than read a book and form opinions about what it takes to be a great surgeon. You would want someone who is practiced at surgery, who has disciplined him or herself toward mastering it. The world around us is in need of God's people, but they need more than Christians with a lot of head knowledge. They need the "leavening yeast" of God's community of transformative love, mature through years of walking with Jesus and learning from him.

My roommate in college became a thoracic surgeon. After he completed his undergraduate degree, he went to four years of medical school, then a general residency for two years, then an additional specialized residency for his surgical specialty. He was required to work so many hours during residency—over one hundred hours per week, while receiving a fixed salary—that his actual hourly earnings were less than minimum wage. He persevered, however, and became a thoracic surgeon with his own practice.

Initially, during his surgical training, he would operate on cadavers so that any mistakes made would not result in a problem. Then he graduated to assisting in surgeries, taking on more and more responsibility until his surgical mentors deemed him ready to go solo. Even then, veteran surgeons mentored him and provided close supervision. He literally apprenticed himself to master surgeons in order to learn how to be a surgeon.

While becoming an apprentice of Jesus is much more than developing a set of competencies the way a novice surgeon does, it does involve discipline, consistent attention, effort, obedience, and an understanding that patience is needed. It requires choosing life instead of "death" on a moment-by-moment basis (Deuteronomy 30:19). It is constantly enhancing life and dignity with others rather than diminishing them through our attitudes, actions, and ways of being.

The goal is not to get to some sort of spiritual plane where you have "arrived." It is to live with increased awareness and intentionality, resulting in generating an ever-increasing impact of love. This requires consistently increasing awareness of your experience, attitudes and impact on others and course correcting when needed. It requires a willingness to own the results you produce in your life rather than blaming them on someone else, the circumstances, or yourself. Simply own them in a non-judgmental way. Then, commit to learn through openness and curiosity rather than resisting your current reality. Take that learning and recalibrate and go again. The need for this will never go away. We are imperfect. God's grace and mercy enables us to grow and connect with him and others anyway.

Love is not a feeling. It can certainly include feelings, and it usually does. But love is a committed action. It is a way of being. It is an orientation. In the New Testament, there are many words for love. For the most part, when referring to love in this study, I am referring to *agape* love—the unconditional love God bestows on us. That is the love he asks us to live as a response to his demonstrated love for us.

The amazing thing is that we have the opportunity to not only be mentored by fellow apprentices in God's community of transformative love (Matthew 28:18–20). We are also directly mentored by Jesus Christ himself through his Spirit dwelling within us. This is the fulfillment of "Christ in you, the hope of glory, which is the riches of the glory of the great mystery"—Colossians 1:27.

There are two key aspects to maturing as an apprentice of Jesus.

1. One is deepening your intimacy and connection with God.

2. The second is awakening to your impact on others, so you can deepen your connection to them.

THE PATH TO DEEPENING YOUR CONNECTION AND INTIMACY WITH GOD: PRAYING WITH WORDS AND PRAYING WITHOUT WORDS

In the Gospels, Jesus instructed us on the basics of being in conversation with God, and the attitude with which to engage him. This is "praying with words." It is engaging God in an ongoing conversation born out of our desire to be close to him, our love for him, and our willingness to stand "naked" before him.

We also have an opportunity to "pray without words." By this, I am referring to practicing stillness in silence and solitude. This also includes contemplative prayer—for example when you attend to your breathing and breathe in God's delight or peace, and exhale your delight in him. You are contemplating those realities in real time in an embodied action. You are praying with your entire being, your breath life, your body as you imagine God's love permeating every cell of your body, and with your heart, as you resonate with his goodness, joy, or peace. You also are using your mind (without words) as you see in your "mind's eye" the love of God flowing into your being as you breathe in.

Praying without words is an embodied prayer. It is praying with your entire body, heart, soul, spirit, and mind. It integrates your heart, soul, mind, and spirit. It directly supports your ability to shift the posture of your heart from attitudes of selfishness to attitudes of goodness and love.

Both praying with words and praying without words are essential means of communication with God as apprentices of Jesus.

AWAKENING TO YOUR IMPACT ON OTHERS—DEEPENING YOUR CONNECTION TO THEM

Another aspect of apprenticing with Jesus is developing an increasing awareness of the impact we have on others. This simply embraces Jesus's directive to love others. It is embracing the current reality of our lives regarding this and allowing that reality to guide us rather than our own subjective, self-flattering views of how loving we are. Who, after all, is the ultimate arbiter of whether or not I am loving another person? Is it not the other?

Jesus Christ mentors us through these efforts in several ways:

- Through the presence of his indwelling spirit,

- Through his actions and teachings during his three-year ministry on earth, chronicled in the Gospels,

- Through his actions throughout history, after his ascension, as he continues to presence himself through the actions of his faithful followers. This includes the Scriptures of the New Testament, as well as the way he has spoken through his followers throughout church history and the way he speaks to us personally as we interact with him.

As we get into the ways of being, attitudes, and actions Jesus instructs his followers to embrace, it is clear that his way of relating was completely countercultural. The culture of the world is upside down in comparison to God's kingdom.

God's plan is to "leaven" the earth with his people and his kingdom (Matthew 3:2, 13:33). Leaven—or yeast—is the key ingredient that makes bread dough rise. It is not the largest ingredient in a loaf of bread, but it is critical to the bread turning out when it is baked.

As apprentices, we revolutionize the earth by transforming the way we show up in our spheres of influence. That includes loved ones, friends, acquaintances, and fellow workers. It also includes people we don't get along with, even enemies. In Matthew 5:44, Jesus tells us to love our enemies and to pray for those that persecute us. That is a radically countercultural mindset. Think about how the world would be different today if we all practiced that. Do you think our political discourse would be different? Jesus doesn't tell us to tell everyone else to shape up, to judge them, and to criticize them when we disagree. He essentially is telling us to own *our* lives and to transform the way *we* are relating. I don't see anywhere in the gospels where he tells his followers to become lecturers of others about how we think they should act, while ignoring their own contributions that miss the mark of love. That is hypocrisy.

In short, our sphere of influence includes anyone with whom we interact with in any way. When you really think about walking this out day by day, it is a sobering reality. The first step to changing the world is to own *your* life, *your* contribution, and *your* impact.

THE HEART OF THE MATTER

Again, here is the signature impact generated by those who apprentice themselves to Jesus:

> Let me give you a new command: Love one another. In the same way I loved you, you love one another. This is how everyone will recognize that you are my disciples—when they see the love you have for each other. (John 13:34–35, MSG)

Jesus unfolded the nature of how this love can revolutionize our lives, both internally and externally:

> Then one of the scribes came, and having heard them reasoning together, perceiving that -He had answered them well, asked Him, "Which is the first commandment of all?" Jesus answered him, "The first of all the commandments is: 'Hear, O Israel, the Lord our God, the Lord is one. And you shall love the Lord your God with all your heart, with all your soul, with all your mind, and with all your strength.' This is the first commandment. And the second, like it, is this: 'You shall love your neighbor as yourself.' There is no other commandment greater than these." (Mark 12:28–31)

BECOMING CHRIST-LIKE APPRENTICE

Becoming Christ-like as an apprentice of Jesus is twofold.

I. EMBRACING GOD'S LOVE FOR US

First, as a natural response to what God has given us through Jesus, we become enthralled, delighted, and in awe of God's love for us, to such a degree that nothing can shake our belief in his undeniable goodness as we love him with our whole being.

Perhaps this sounds obvious to you. But the boldness, freedom, passion, and power that putting this into practice infuses into our lives is the true indicator of how much we have embraced it.

First John 4:7–9 tells us to "Love one another, for love is of God; and everyone who loves is born of God and knows God. He who does not love does not know God, for God is love. In this the love of God was manifested toward us, that God has sent His only begotten Son into the world, that we might live through Him."

The foundation of this complete love and devotion to God that we are called to is an unshakeable belief in God's goodness. 1 John 1:5 tells us that "God is light and in him is no darkness at all." God's goodness leads us to repentance (Romans 2:4). The covering that his goodness generates enables us to actually look at the areas of our lives that are not aligned in love and goodness so that we can change how we live.

Our fear of engaging the stark truth of the fallen nature of our lives, fearing failure, rejection, vulnerability, or shame, is overcome through an unequivocal belief in God's goodness—that he can actually be trusted in the most difficult and vulnerable areas of our lives. The realization that he is absolutely good and light and has no darkness at all, makes it possible to trust him enough to come out of hiding and to stop concealing our sin and pain in the deep recesses of our souls.

God may not seem safe when viewed in the upside-down context of our culture, but he is safe even when it doesn't feel that way. For that matter, he is already with us where we hide—nothing we can reveal will drive him away. Even when we can't see, sense, feel, or experience him, he is present in the dark places where we feel abandoned.

In the Old Testament, Israel's King David was called a man after God's own heart, although he committed some horrible mistakes in his life, including adultery and murder. If you read the psalms David wrote, and the account of his life in the books of 1 and 2 Samuel, one thing becomes unmistakably clear: David was passionately in love with God and completely naked before him. He pleaded with God, adored him, praised him, implored him, and bared his soul before him. He owned his mistakes and asked God's forgiveness. He was all-out in his devotion to and service for his God. What an example for us to follow as apprentices of Jesus!

2. EXTENDING GOD'S LOVE FOR OUR NEIGHBORS

Second, we learn to love our neighbor as ourselves. This is a significant aspect of becoming Christ-like. The word "neighbor" in Mark 12:31 refers to those who are nearby as we walk through our daily lives. In other words, love the one(s) you're with, even if they are your enemies (Matthew 5:43–44). Jesus says to love them "as yourself."

Not only is Jesus instructing us to extend loving-kindness and appreciation toward ourselves—thus embracing God's view of us—he is asking us to extend loving-kindness toward all those around us.

In today's narcissistic "self-esteem" culture, this can get confusing. Extending loving-kindness and appreciation toward yourself is distinct from simply having an inflated view of yourself and denying your negative impact on others by saying you are a "good person" or otherwise pumping yourself up. The type of loving-kindness we extend to ourselves is a humility, deep gratitude, and awareness of God's grace (unmerited favor) and mercy (withholding of merited judgment). And that gratitude and appreciation is the foundation for how and why we extend grace and mercy to others. That attitude and posture of heart is what Jesus is referring to here. As C.S. Lewis says in *Mere Christianity,* "True humility is not thinking less of yourself; it is thinking of yourself less."

This study for Christlikeness we are engaging as apprentices of Jesus will continually come back to the nuances and deep work of the twofold pursuit of becoming Christ-like—embracing God's love for us and expressing the love of God to others. We will never get to the bottom of all the possibilities, because they are infinite. At any point in our lives, no matter how much spiritual maturity we have developed as apprentices, we will only be scratching the surface of the reality of the love of God. This is good news, not bad news. It means there is always hope, always a deeper awareness and expression of God's love to be discovered, no matter how challenging the situation or how difficult the person.

This truly is the ultimate adventure. And it is the ultimate challenge. It is the price of admission to becoming an apprentice of Jesus. The call to love applies even to people in your life whom you think are unlovable. In fact, it especially applies to them. They are your gift from God to call you into deeper waters of expressing your love.

APPRENTICING WITH JESUS THROUGH PRAYER: THE POWER OF REQUEST

In Luke 11:9–10, Jesus tells his disciples, "So I say to you: Ask and it will be given to you; seek and you will find; knock and the door will be opened to you. For everyone who asks receives; the one who seeks finds; and to the one who knocks, the door will be opened."

When we embrace the love of God for us in humility, acknowledging how much he cares for us and how much we need him, we discover a natural part of living in conversation with God: the role and power of request. Over fifteen times in the Gospels, Jesus reiterates the critical nature of the power of request when in conversation/prayer with his heavenly Father.

- He tells them God knows what they need even before they ask (Matthew 6:8).

- He tells them the key to receiving from God *is to ask* (Matthew 7:7–11, 21:22; Luke 11:9–13; John 14:13–14).

- He reveals some important keys to empowering request, namely abiding in him and asking in his name (John 14:13–14; 15:7, 16; 16:23–26).

- He emphasizes that believing—faith—is key (Mark 11:24).

- He teaches that praying in agreement with another is a powerful form of request (Matthew 18:19).

Some have turned these magnificent promises into what I call the "God as my personal butler" way of relating. It is no surprise that in our narcissistic, instant-gratification culture, this way of relating to God exists. James 4 provides tremendous clarity regarding this:

What causes fights and quarrels among you? Don't they come from your desires that battle within you? You desire but do not have, so you kill. You covet but you cannot get what you want, so you quarrel and fight. You do not have because you do not ask God. When you ask, you do not receive, because you ask with wrong motives, that you may spend what you get on your pleasures.

You adulterous people, don't you know that friendship with the world means enmity against God? Therefore, anyone who chooses to be a friend of the world becomes an enemy of God. Or do you think Scripture says without reason that he jealously longs for the spirit he has caused to dwell in us? But he gives us more grace. That is why Scripture says:

"God opposes the proud, but shows favor to the humble." (James 4:1–6, NIV)

It is not simply the action taken, but *who we are in the doing of the action* that makes the difference. If our requests in prayer are from the point of view of our consumerist, impatient, instant-results-demanding, narcissistic culture, we will be disappointed in our expectations. We are not to be petulant children, throwing tantrums or withdrawing when God doesn't answer the way we want. However, if our requests come from an attitude of humility, openness, and curiosity, then we enter a completely different realm of possibility.

WHEN GOD ANSWERS

John Gottman, the well-known author and marriage researcher, has said that the majority of marital issues are never fully resolved. What I take from this is that getting my way must not be the key to a healthy marriage, because on many, many issues, I am simply not going to get my preference. Certainly, that is true in virtually all of our relationships. People simply do not show up the way we prefer very often.

If this is true in human relationship, how is it that we so often take a completely different tack with God in prayer? We pray, and if the answer is not quickly forthcoming or evident within a "reasonable" period of time, we either doubt ourselves or doubt God's presence and trustworthiness rather than staying in the conversation.

In Isaiah 5:8–9, NIV God says, "For my thoughts are not your thoughts, neither are your ways my ways." God has an entirely new way of relating in store for those who stay in the conversation with him—who notice that he does not line up with their preferences often but who stick with him anyway.

God's answers may often not match our preferences or expectations. He rarely answers in a way that is immediately discernable. Rather than withdrawing in disappointment or demanding something different, take the times your expectations and God's answers differ as an opportunity to learn a new way of relating and embrace it with curiosity.

> Mother Teresa was once asked, "When you pray, what do you say to God?" She said, "I don't talk, I listen." The interviewer then asked: "What does God say to you?" Mother Teresa replied, "He doesn't talk. He listens. And if you don't understand that, I can't explain it to you."
>
> Another time, she said, "Prayer is not asking. Prayer is putting oneself in the hands of God, at His disposition, and listening to His voice in the depth of our hearts."

Our relationship with God is not based on transactions. It is not rooted in me simply making a request and God answering. It is rooted first in intimacy. We rest and immerse ourselves in his presence. Mother Teresa's answers reveal the importance of intimacy and contemplation in a vibrant prayer life. Contemplation allows us the opportunity to get beyond our preset expectations and imagine what is beyond them as we sit in silence and remain open to God's presence and promptings.

The foundation is intimacy with God. When requests come from that orientation, our expectations shift from self-focus to discovery and new awareness.

THE HUMILITY OF REQUESTS

The very act of making a request of another requires humility. What is the difference between a request and a demand? When you make a request of another, you are acknowledging that the possibility of it happening is in the other person's hands to grant, not grant, or negotiate.

God's request of us is that we utilize the power of request in our conversations with him. He desires that we make requests with childlike confidence and trust in his goodness. To expect God to do things for you without humbly making requests is entitled, arrogant, and haughty. God lays out this amazing smorgasbord of possibility before all people, but so many fail to make a simple request. And then these people curse God or, at the very least mistrust him, because their lives are not what they desire. That is entitled insanity within the kingdom of heaven.

Prayer flows out of an ongoing conversation with a God who loves us. That is the reason for requests and the context in which they can be offered joyfully, humbly, and openly.

All prayer is based on the foundation of requests. There are other types of prayer, such as the prayer of praise, the prayer of worship, and the prayer of celebration. And yet, the foundation of request underlies them all. They all are undergirded by a desire for God to make himself known to us, to be with us in deep connection.

THE IMPORTANCE OF NEGOTIATION

When you make a request of a friend, spouse, child, or important associate, and they are not fully on board with your request, what do you say? If you feel freedom to fully engage in that relationship, often you will engage in a negotiation to reach an answer that works for both of you.

This level of intimacy, connection, and awareness is also available with God. However, a level of clarity is required as to God's purposes and how to engage with him—a level of clarity built on the foundation we have been emphasizing in the contemplative disciplines.

In Genesis 18:22–33, Abraham negotiates with God, requesting that he not destroy Sodom and Gomorrah for their sin. First he gets agreement from God not to destroy the cities if fifty righteous people are in them. Then Abraham proceeds to negotiate that number down to forty-five, then forty, then thirty, then twenty, and finally only ten. If ten righteous people were found, God would not destroy the cities. Amazing! I don't think it would naturally occur to me to engage God with that kind of back and forth, yet he clearly was open to it in his conversation with Abraham.

92

In Genesis 32:24–32, Jacob wrestled with an angel and insisted that God bless him, and God ultimately did. In Numbers 11, Moses negotiated with God over getting additional help in his responsibilities. In Numbers 14, God said he was going to destroy Israel due to their idolatry, and Moses negotiated for their lives. God relented and pardoned Israel as a result of Moses's stand and negotiation with him. In 2 Kings 20, King Hezekiah was dying, and he negotiated with God for an additional fifteen years of life.

There are multiple accounts in the Gospels where socially marginalized people—usually women—negotiated with Jesus to receive blessings of various kinds and were granted those blessings. And Jesus himself negotiated with God in Luke 22:39–46, asking him to take from him his upcoming crucifixion and death, yet God could not grant that request.

This is a "both-and" consideration…not "either-or." Yes, the foundation of our prayer life is learning to practice stillness so that we can be intimate with and know God. In addition, prayer can be an ongoing, active conversation with God, bringing our entire heart before him—holding nothing back.

The point in all this is that God desires that we bring all of what we have into our relationship with him. He desires that we engage him, wrestle with him if need be, and work together in a passionate, committed way.

This clearly doesn't mean every answer to prayer will match our initial preference. But it does mean that God desires for us to fully engage in our conversations with him as his people.

ANSWERS TO PRAYER

Perhaps God has not always answered your prayers in the manner you desired. But is that different from any other relationship? Doesn't any healthy relationship include a willingness to be honest about what is true for you, to speak it, and to hear the other out? Aren't we always called to be flexible and to create elegant solutions together when we are not on the same page? Doesn't it require generous listening to be able to hear the other's heart and to include it in your thinking and consideration? Why would it be any different with God?

Oswald Chambers wrote:

> God never speaks to us in startling ways, but in ways that are easy to misunderstand, and we say, "I wonder if that is God's voice?" Isaiah said that the Lord spoke to him "with a strong hand," that is, by the pressure of circumstances. Nothing touches our lives but it is God Himself speaking. Do we discern His hand or mere occurrence? Get into the habit of saying, "Speak Lord," and life will become a romance. Every time circumstances press you, say "Speak Lord"; make time to listen.[29]

Many times, for me, it is easier to see God's hand and his answers to prayer by looking back on occurrences as I walk ahead in faith. Often the hand of God becomes clearer by looking at what he has produced in our lives. These things can easily go unnoticed if we are not attuned to his workings and trusting him to be in the conversation of prayer with us. However God works with you, the point is that prayer is the primary expression of your love relationship with God. It is the conversation of the beloved with he who is love.[30]

STILLNESS AND CONVERSATION WITH GOD

Continue to practice stillness in silence and solitude, and then practice being in a conversation with God that includes requests.

"Be still, and know that I am God."—Psalm 46:10a, NIV

"Come to me, all you who are weary and burdened and I will give you rest. Take my yoke upon you and learn from me, for I am gentle and humble in heart, and you will find rest for your souls. For my yoke is easy and my burden is light." — Matthew 11:28–30, NIV

PRACTICING STILLNESS

For this set of practices, you are going to again start by practicing stillness, using breathing as the mechanism to quiet yourself. Every time you practice these contemplative disciplines, you start with practicing stillness. It is an amazingly restful practice in and of itself. And, it also quiets the mind to prepare it for *contemplating God's presence and resting and abiding in his presence.*

After practicing stillness, here is a simple way to practice being in a conversation with God using words and silence:

Get in a quiet place, with no distractions. You want to also practice the spiritual disciplines of silence and solitude as you engage practicing stillness.

You can practice this sitting, laying down, or walking. Your choice… whatever supports you being able to focus best. If you are sitting, sit with your back straight and your feet flat on the floor. If you are lying down, lie is a comfortable pose. If you are walking, walk with your head level, back straight and looking ahead.

- Close your eyes (unless you are walking), and start paying attention to your breathing. Deeply inhale through your nose all the way deep into your belly. Your stomach should go out as you inhale. Exhale through your mouth. Focus on your breath as you inhale and as you exhale.

- Calm your mind and release the constant chatter of your mind by attending to your breathing. See your breath go in and out in your mind's eye. Your mind may not want to calm down. You may have difficulty releasing the need to think thoughts. This is all perfectly normal and no problem at all. The important thing is to simply bring your attention back to your breathing when you do notice your mind wandering.

- The two most important attitudes to practice this with are PATIENCE and NON-JUDGMENT. Practice this always with patience and non-judgmentally. To practice non-judgmentally is to be accepting of whatever is. In other words, even if your mind wanders all the time, you do not judge yourself for not doing it well, you simply notice it, and bring your mind back without resisting that this occurred.

- When you are practicing stillness, you are observing with love—not with resistance, judgment, analysis, or labeling—just observation with love and reverence.

- Turn your attention inward and notice your physical sensations and feelings. Just notice them. Do not feel compelled to do anything about them.

- Do this for at least a few minutes per day. In the beginning, two minutes is a win, and twelve minutes is a home run. Ultimately you will want to expand the time you do this. It is a delightful experience to simply be still and PRACTICE stillness. It sets the stage for a deeper experience of God and yourself.

Now, in addition to practicing stillness, you can practice conversing with God, including making requests. You may want to review the sections towards the end of the just concluded chapter.

- *Consider the specifics of the vision you are pursuing* in relation to this *Apprenticing Jesus* study.

- *Identify the areas of that vision in which you feel stuck* or are not experiencing the transformational movement you desire.

- After you have quieted yourself and become present through practicing stillness, *your contemplation and prayer time is going to focus on these areas you have identified. It is time to have a conversation with God about it.*

Throughout this contemplative prayer time, continue to attend to your deep breathing and stay aware of your body's internal state. When your mind wanders from the conversation at hand, simply bring it back to focus on the specific area you are discussing.

Then, as you continue to breathe deeply and attend to your breathing:

- Bring to mind the first area of your vision you desire more movement in. For now, that is all you are going to focus on. Be patient and take your time. Focus on only one specific area at a time.

- Understand that the goal is not to get this figured out immediately. The goal is to start an ongoing conversation with God about it—a conversation with words and without words.

- Continue this for however much time you have to practice it. Don't worry about whether it "is working" or not. Simply practice it and enjoy practicing the presence of God—within you and all around you—bathing you in his love and peace. Even if you are not feeling it, simply practice its presence.

- Think of what requests you have of God regarding your topic. For example, I am currently working on a large project that I have been working on for several years. I am currently not sure what next steps to take to move the project forward. So, in my prayer time, I am asking God to give me wisdom and to make clear the path forward.

    o I make that request by speaking to him.

    o I also make that request without words. I do this contemplatively—by breathing in his wisdom regarding this and breathing out my gratitude for his guidance. I may breathe out my trust in him showing me the way, breathe out any anxiety, or breathing out any doubt or frustration I may feel.

    o I am not concerned with whether I hear or notice anything discernable from God in that moment. Maybe I do or maybe I don't. Usually I don't. I am not concerned with the timing. I know God is on his own timetable and he will reveal what he reveals in the way he chooses to reveal it when he desires to do so. In the meantime, I get to stay in a conversation with him, perhaps even negotiating what I think I am hearing from him.

o There are many ways to hear from God. Scripture talks about a still small voice (1 Kings 9:12). For some it is simply a knowing. For others, it is a progressive step-by-step process, based on what they think they are hearing or even what they hear from God audibly at times. That is extremely rare for me, if ever. Just be in the conversation and practice releasing extraneous thoughts when they intervene into your focused presence with God.

• Spend as much time as you have allocated for this, and end by thanking God for his goodness and faithfulness.

CHAPTER 7

THE SPIRITUAL PRACTICE OF AUTHENTICITY

If you are walking through this study with a small group or with friends, you have a unique opportunity to take new ground in your commitment to authenticity, transparency, vulnerability, and intimacy with each other. Of course, that requires uncommon courage, openness, and honesty. But it is the necessary path toward experiencing your true self in a new and profound way.

Being authentic is being true about 'what is so' for you for the purpose of creating connection and care with another.

Being authentic breaks through our natural tendency to hide, to avoid, and to project the image we think will get us through while masking what is actually true for us.

ENGAGING YOUR VISION

Where in your life are you being less than fully authentic? Maybe you are simply not saying or owning what is so for you. Maybe you are withholding or misrepresenting what is really so for you. How is this impacting your vision for this study? This week is a great opportunity to embrace authenticity and the freedom it brings.

In Romans 12:9, we are told to "Love without hypocrisy" (ASV). The word "hypocrisy" in this verse literally means to play a part—to wear a mask. Often we are not even aware of the survival strategies we run to get through life—strategies that started when we were young. It never ceases to amaze me how blind we can be to our own "stuff."

Unawareness is one of the great challenges in becoming Christ-like. During our time in this journey, we will continually explore how to create increased awareness of our impact on others. This consideration can also lead to identifying your largely unconscious attitudes that contribute to impacts that are incongruent with our stated intentions.

1 Corinthians 13:12 states that our experience of life is like looking at puzzling reflections in a mirror. In those days, mirrors were very flawed and always reflected a distorted image of whoever was looking in them. The King James Version of this verse referred to it as "looking through a glass darkly." *The Message* refers to it as "squinting in a fog, peering through a mist."

The time will come when Jesus returns, as expressed in Thessalonians and Revelation, when we will see clearly and know as God fully knows us. But in the meantime, being born into an imperfect world with an imperfect nature, we do not ever see reality with complete clarity. We need to interrupt our own unawareness so that we can learn to see in new ways.

INTERRUPTING UNAWARENESS

We can interrupt our lack of awareness—of clarity—in three primary ways.

First, be intentionally aware of your own inner space. We tend to be unaware of this crucial aspect of ourselves. By "inner space" I am referring to your inner being—what you are experiencing, feeling, and sensing, both physically and emotionally.

One of the most important aspects of the spiritual disciplines, including silence and stillness, is that they turn your attention inward—as you follow your breath, as you inhale and exhale. These disciplines allow you to clear your normal thoughts and thinking processes and start noticing what is actually going on inside of you as you are simply present—paying attention on purpose, nonjudgmentally, in the present moment.

This is a beginning step and ongoing discipline that allows you to develop an inner awareness, the rich ground in which spiritual awareness can be grown. If God instructs us to be still so that we can know he is God, does it not behoove us to establish new levels of inner awareness in order to enrich our overall awareness of him, as well as ourselves, and—ultimately—others?

Second, be intentionally aware of the impact you have on others. We tend to be unaware of this as well. Your inner awareness has a direct impact on your "other awareness." If I am oblivious of the motives, attitudes, emotions, and inner sensations that drive me, it follows that I am going to be equally oblivious of how those unknown internal motivators influence my actions and way of being and thus spill over to influence others. That is why self-refection is so important: it can lead to adjustments that increase our awareness of others.

Neuroscientists refer to this inner observation/self-reflection as "mindfulness." When that is reflected toward another, increasing our ability to walk in empathy, compassion, and love, neuroscientists refer to it as "mindsight."

Volumes of books are being written on the specifics of these dynamics. For our purposes right now, just consider that you are not fully aware of the impact you are having on others. You see this reality "through a glass darkly." You never have the full score. This underscores the importance of creating agreements in relationships that allow each of you to be honest about how you impact each other.

Third, interrupt your inflated view of your positive impact on others. This view is primarily due to basing your self-assessment on your conscious good intentions. I have heard it said that people have two possible views of themselves: one is inflated, and the other is pure fantasy. We rarely take into consideration our underlying, unconscious, survival-based intentions, yet they leak through in our actions and words, often undercutting the impact we aspire to have.

An inflated view of self can apply to self-loathing also, which is a negatively inflated view. Self-loathing is simply the flip side of fantasy-based "self-esteem."

Psalm 139:23–24, NIV says, "Search me, God, and know my heart; test me and know my anxious thoughts. See if there is any offensive way in me, and lead me in the way everlasting." Lamentations 3:40, NIV tells us to "examine our ways and test them."

WHAT GETS IN THE WAY OF AWARENESS

Jeremiah says, "The heart is deceitful above all things, and desperately wicked, who can know it?" (17:9, NIV). In the next verse, God gives tremendous insight as to how he negotiates this human reality and how we can emulate him. He says he "searches the heart, and examines the mind, to reward each person according to their conduct, according to what their deeds deserve" 17:10, NIV)

The Message translation of these two verses sums it up beautifully: "The heart is hopelessly dark and deceitful, a puzzle that no one can figure out. But I, God, search the heart and examine the mind. I get to the heart of the human. I get to the root of things. I treat them as they really are, not as they pretend to be."

God notices our deeds and our conduct, i.e., the results we create, the impacts we have, and the behaviors we display by noticing our actions and what we say. "Out of the abundance of the heart, the mouth speaks" (Matthew 12:34). That cuts through much of the confusion and deceit. It pierces the inflated view of self that contributes so strongly to not seeing the reality of the impact of our lives (Romans 12:3).

Over time, we will continue to unfold multiple spiritual practices and disciplines to support you in this process of becoming aware. These practices, such as examining and testing your ways, will help you turn your heart toward God (Lamentations 3:40). For now, simply consider the value of transparency.

John 8:32 tells us that truth—reality—will set us free. Fantasy, self-deceit, and inflated views of self will never lead us to freedom. They only produce bondage.

A commitment to transparency is an invitation to start noticing what you previously did not notice in terms of your attitudes, assumptions, judgments, beliefs, and actions. Human nature (or "the old man" or "sin nature" or "the flesh"—these phrases are all basically synonymous) is to minimize, defend, or dismiss these things. Yet Jesus asks us to *embrace the reality of our current life* as the starting point for moving toward true freedom. Rather than resisting reality because it does not line up with what we prefer, he asks us to experientially connect to it.

The word for "know" in John 8:32 ("and you will *know* the truth") means to "know experientially." Not to merely know intellectually, but to be connected to what we are experiencing in our current reality—our thoughts, feelings, emotions, physical sensations, and experience of living.

The great Danish philosopher, from the 1800's, Soren Kierkegaard wrote, "To see yourself is to die to all illusions and all hypocrisy. It takes great courage to dare to look at yourself—something that can take place only in the mirror of the Word. You must want only the truth, neither vainly wish to be flattered nor self-tormentingly want to be made pure devil."

Looking at yourself in this manner and being transparent interrupts avoidance, resistance, and hiding. It creates a powerful opportunity to work with whatever is there and transition through it.

> This is the message we have heard from him and declare to you: God is light; in him there is no darkness at all. If we claim to have fellowship with him and yet walk in the darkness, we lie and do not live out the truth. But if we walk in the light, as he is in the light, we have fellowship with one another, and the blood of Jesus, his Son, purifies us from all sin. If we claim to be without sin, we deceive ourselves and the truth is not in us. If we confess our sins, he is faithful and just and will forgive us our sins and purify us from all unrighteousness. If we claim we have not sinned, we make him out to be a liar and his word is not in us. (1 John 1:5–10, NIV)

The promise of walking in the light is profound. It generates connection (fellowship with one another), freedom (as we are purified from sin and unrighteousness), and forgiveness. It leads the way out of self-deceit and living a lie. It is the pathway to authenticity and being true.

RESISTING YOUR CURRENT REALITY

As you apprentice with Jesus and especially as you work on growing your awareness, notice when you are resisting your current reality. By current reality, I mean the sum total of your present life—the status of your key relationships, the state of mind you are in, whether you are accomplishing what you desire, your internal emotional state, your peace of mind (or lack thereof), your level of calmness (or the opposite—busyness), your inner awareness and awareness of others, and your view of the world around you, both close to you and far away from you.

We resist our current reality when it does not match up with what we prefer. Usually, that resistance is manifested when we conclude that something is wrong with us, with someone else, or with the situation we are in. Notice when you are playing this blame game. Notice, too, when you are unwilling to be open and honest about what is happening for you. That is simply another form of resistance to current reality. Commit to bringing this resistance out into the open, with your small group, and/or those you are in relationship with. Be willing to own your humanity, knowing that God will forgive any shortcomings, if you ask his forgiveness. All you need to do is ask.

Transparency and authenticity can be for the benefit of serving and caring and creating connection with others, but they can also be self-serving. Your motive in sharing will determine the fruit that action creates. The more quickly and fully you are willing to "get real" during this journey, the more quickly you will be able to gain clarity regarding your motives and create a possibility for change, growth, and transformation.

NOTICE THE WAYS YOU AVOID

We humans employ sophisticated mechanisms to avoid things we don't want to deal with. This might look like procrastinating, hiding, day-dreaming, overanalyzing, judging, sleeping, criticizing, lying, arguing, making excuses, minimizing, giving the silent treatment, chitchatting, intellectualizing, playing it safe, joking, defending, blaming, quitting, drinking or binging, overeating, drugs, or knowing it all (or thinking you know it all, anyway). And that's just to name a few!

You may notice some of these coming up for you as you continue to engage this journey. When you notice an avoidance tactic kicking in, you can choose to release it, be courageous, and participate fully. For example, if I notice myself minimizing a consideration—rendering it unnecessary or not worth putting time into—I can choose to release the need to minimize and instead be open to whatever is there for me to learn. I release minimizing, and instead choose openness.

NOTICE WHAT YOU RESIST

As you engage this journey, notice what you resist. All the ways of avoiding mentioned above are forms of resistance. *Resistance is an automatic response to any input or situation we feel threatens our physical, emotional, or spiritual well-being or survival.* For example, if we see a bear in the woods, we will typically run away to preserve our physical safety from this threat to our well-being. But often, rather than a real threat to our physical well-being, our impulse is for the survival of our identity and ego. We unconsciously sense existential threats when something happens that makes us feel vulnerable.

A close friend of mine feels that his survival mechanism kicks in when he's around anyone similar to him whom he deems more successful or intelligent or just plain "better" than himself. He wants to start belittling them (defensiveness) or else beating himself up (shame) because he feels threatened. Then he'll resist being with them or around them to make those feelings go away. But when my friend brings his insecurities and resistance to God, he realizes that he's not trusting that God's love and goodness are enough, and that reminds him to stop resisting and to trust God instead.

I notice resistance in myself when life isn't going the way I prefer. If my wife, Katie, isn't behaving the way I want, I notice that I want to withdraw (avoidance) or judge her (make her wrong). When I do that, the situation just escalates and persists. It either gets worse or stays below the surface, influencing our interactions. If I interrupt these unhelpful attitudes with care, curiosity, and empathy, the situation almost always quickly resolves itself.

We tend to resist anything that threatens our ability to be right, in control, comfortable or safe. We want to feel good or look good. Any time you notice internal resistance—as you work through this study and as you apprentice with Jesus in your daily life—intentionally think about why you are feeling threatened, identify the reason, and then meet that resistance with a willingness to consider whatever generated it. That sounds very theoretical, but the application is quite practical.

Throughout this study, we are exploring practical ways that you can stop resisting and start surrendering. This happens as we enter conversation with God authentically and openly, and it happens as we practice spiritual disciplines of silence, solitude, and stillness. By "surrendering" I do not mean resigning or giving up. I mean simply accepting the reality of what *is* as a starting point for where you are as you determine what is *next*. Surrender is about releasing resistance because your current reality is not what you prefer, and embracing it as a provision rather than as a problem.

AWARENESS AND YOUR DAILY PRAYER TIME

Your daily prayer time in silence and solitude is an opportunity to be "naked" before God—to be in his presence while you are present in whatever you are sensing, noticing, feeling, and experiencing, with no felt need to "fix" it. Simply be with him in it, honoring him with your intimacy and openness before him.

Apprenticing with Jesus requires full participation. What does that look like? Being fully engaged, open, honest, vulnerable, willing to "live in the question." Rather than quickly skipping through your questions and considerations, be willing to look beyond your current set of assumptions, assessments, judgments, opinions, and beliefs about yourself, others, and life. Be willing to consider and own your contribution to breakdowns in your life rather than minimizing and dismissing it. "Living in the question" is an invitation to stay open and curious, seeing beyond what is immediately obvious. It is an invitation to self-observe and self-reflect, to provide an opportunity for new awareness to bubble up to the surface of your thoughts from your sub-conscious.

In your daily time with God, be willing to openly ponder and reflect and observe where an inquiry leads you. Marinate in the question. Consider it ongoing. This is huge. The practice of nonjudgmentally, reflectively observing yourself and what makes you tick is a fundamental transformational discipline. This practice saves you from simply being caught up in your own responses without really considering or noticing them.

Full participation also includes a deep commitment to action. There is a vast difference between knowing information and living it. Reflection can be a powerful exercise that results in new insights. But unless you act on those insights, you are simply engaged in "navel-gazing" and won't see much of a difference in your life.

Having a deep commitment to action, however, does not mean that you should be in continual motion. Quite the opposite. Creating space for God through the spiritual disciplines of silence, solitude, stillness, contemplation, and prayer are foundational for taking effective action in life.

TAKE THE POSTURE OF A LEARNER, NOT A KNOWER

For the first half of my adult life, I thought the key to living an effective life was to ascertain the keys to life. I prided myself on learning and knowing as much as possible. Eventually I realized that, for me, this produced arrogance based on what I knew and believed to be true.

I will never forget when that realization hit me. It crushed me. I started seeing how many people I had missed in my life and how much value from others I had missed because their beliefs did not line up with mine.

Jesus said that adopting the posture and mind-set of a child is a prerequisite for entering the kingdom of heaven (Matthew 18:3,4). Young children are curious, hungry to learn, and continually asking for more. Adopting a "learner posture" versus a "knower posture" is essential to gain the most from your journey.

Knowledge is not the key to powerful and effective living, nor is it the key to apprenticing with Jesus. There are no set formulas for loving others.

Learning tends to cease when I decide that I know what is needed in a particular area of life. My natural curiosity to notice what is beyond what I currently see diminishes. Maintaining the discipline of patient curiosity, wonder, and awe in the learning process is a powerful support toward taking effective action in what you are learning.

In this journey of apprenticing with Jesus, we are consistently invited to be curious—to live in the question. This means interrupting the temptation to come up with quick answers or to quickly adopt or reject the principles we come across in the Scriptures, in this study, and in conversation with God. It might mean becoming willing to not have the answer. Instead, we have the opportunity to consider with an open mind what God might be speaking to us.

Be open to the possibility of discovering what you are currently not seeing. Invite others into your thinking and reflecting so you can learn from their perspectives. When you notice yourself resisting, avoiding, or being unwilling to consider something, ask yourself, "Why am I resisting, avoiding, or unwilling to consider this? What is it I don't know that God is leading me to discover?"

What you do or do not consider is your choice, but living in the question is a powerful way to uncover undiscovered possibilities that God is making available to you.

PATIENCE IS A VIRTUE

One of the great discoveries in recent neuroscience research is that the brain is capable of dramatic growth and change. This is called *neuroplasticity,* the process of developing new neural pathways in the brain.

It is clear from Scripture that God authored this ability. We can be transformed by the renewing of our minds (Romans 12:2). Dramatic, fundamental, radical change is possible. Neurologically, this involves building new neural pathways through consistent action, thoughts, and beliefs. But the new pathway takes some time to build.

Take road building as a metaphor for this process. When a new bypass superhighway is being built, as an alternative to the existing highway, it takes time. The old route usually will still be used during the new bypass construction and after. Building new neural pathways in your brain follows a similar course. While you are building those new "superhighway" pathways that will enable you to be less reliant on old, ineffective attitudes, actions, and ways of relating, you will probably notice that the path of least resistance is to fall into the old ways, the still existing highways in your brain, built by your standard habitual ways of relating. If you build a new neural pathway as an option, the old neural pathway does not go away. But, now you have a solid alternate path. This takes time. While you can start noticing results as you engage this, it also is the work of a lifetime.

The key word to remember as you engage this journey is *patience.* Patience is the cardinal virtue for becoming a disciple. Our culture tries to sell us the latest and greatest thing before moving on, sometimes minutes later, to the next craze. We live in a world of the instant, the now, the "my way." But the Jesus way takes time. He seems to delight in a deliberate, intentional pace—a slow pace, even—where relationship deepens, and change is sustainable and long lasting. While we never "arrive," we can grow and mature if we persist and are patient.

Be patient with yourself. Be in this journey for the long term. If you notice yourself falling off your intended path, simply notice it, and without self-judgment or condemnation, redirect yourself to the new actions, attitudes, and ways of relating you are committed to building. Be patient. Stay the course. Enjoy the journey.

PRAYER AND CONTEMPLATION

While the practices of silence, solitude, and stillness can generate tremendous value in and of themselves, they are also an excellent preparation of your mind, body, and soul for the spiritual discipline of *contemplation*. Together, these disciplines generate awareness in life of yourself, of God, and of what God may be saying to you. This in turn supports your ability to be authentic, to be aware to what is true for you because they create greater self-awareness. This, in turn, creates a path to deeper awareness of others, and how you impact others.

In a general sense, contemplation can focus on one object or idea or person or principle or thought. It also can simply focus on your internal state—what you are feeling, physical sensations, your state of being, without focusing on anything but noticing your felt sensations and experience. As you do this, you may gain new awareness of what you are experiencing, new ideas, different trains of thought, or images related to what you are contemplating.

Contemplation can use an infinite number of areas of focus. You can focus on a work of art and contemplate what it reveals. You can focus on a picture of Jesus or God and contemplate what it reveals. You can contemplate a verse, or a portion of a verse, and then, not presupposing what will come to mind, stay open to what comes up for you regarding it. You can also focus on a person or group or ideal. When contemplating, you choose to reduce the mental chatter that normally runs in your mind. You adopt an 'open slate' regarding whatever you are contemplating and simply notice what bubbles up to the surface of your conscious mind as you clear the normal endless chatter.

Contemplation does not presuppose what is present, and it does not seek to fill "empty space" regarding whatever you are contemplating. It is being purposeful about clearing extraneous thought and simply being present with whatever you are contemplating, noticing what comes up, including your experience, feelings, and bodily sensations.

Contemplative prayer is one form of contemplation—taking a prayer point, then contemplating what God would have you see, be, and do regarding that prayer focus. It is an amazingly powerful form of prayer, generating the possibility of deep spiritual connection. This is what we were doing in a previous chapter with the Apprentice's Prayer (aka Lord's prayer). We focused on one phrase of the Lord's Prayer and then simply noticed what occurred to us regarding it. Using your breath and paying attention to your breath as you inhale and exhale is the mechanism to use to switch your focus from the normal mental chatter to your breathing. This enables you to clear your mind and to see what you notice when you are being intentionally present.

As mentioned in previous chapters, your options for how you engage this are almost unlimited. Often, when I am attending to breathing during silence and solitude, I will envision breathing in the Spirit of God and exhaling (releasing) my flawed nature. Or I breathe in God's love and exhale old judgments of others and myself. Or I inhale God's love and exhale love and kindness to those closest to me and others who come to mind. Or I inhale God's healing power and exhale that healing power toward friends who are sick. Or I inhale gratitude and exhale resentment. Or I inhale gratitude and exhale gratitude. Or I inhale peace and rest and exhale tiredness, or anxiety or stress.

All of this is occurring in my mind's eye while my eyes are closed. If I am sick, I inhale God's healing power and exhale all sources of the sickness from my body. If I notice tension in my body, I follow the breath as it goes into my body to a relaxed area close to the tension, and I envision the relaxed area unraveling the tensed area into relaxation as I exhale and inhale again. These are examples of "prayer without words."

PRACTICING THE DISCIPLINES

Practicing the disciplines we have been exploring in this study—of silence, solitude, stillness, contemplation, and prayer—within the context of attending to breathing is a powerful start toward an inner spiritual experience with God. It increases connection to and awareness of the Christ within. It calms the mind and body, increasing your awareness of the feelings and sensations in your body and your emotions. It grounds you in stillness and quietness.

God usually speaks through a still small voice (1 Kings 19:11–13). Silence and solitude, with their attendant practices of stillness, contemplation, and prayer, help prepare our hearts, minds, and souls to be attuned to his Spirit.

Contemplation is also powerful when reading Scripture and then considering what God is speaking to us through it. This involves reading a Scripture passage during your time of silence and solitude and then contemplating what God is saying to you through it that day.

Taking time out of your daily schedule to engage these disciplines can lay the foundation for transforming your life and character. Since I started engaging these disciplines on a daily basis, I have been amazed at the difference it has made in my life. It has grounded me, generating calm, peace, and patience, confidence in God's hand in my life, and an increased awareness of what is working and not working in my commitment to be a follower of Jesus. It has completely revolutionized my prayer life...both prayer with words and prayer without words.

The key is to just do it. Don't be concerned with whether you are doing it well. Don't be concerned if your mind wanders or you get distracted. Just practice it. It is a PRACTICE. Always practice it non-judgmentally, meaning do not beat yourself up if you think you are not doing it well. That is simple resistance. Being okay with however you are doing it is practicing being present in God's love and acceptance. You cannot mess this up. Simply practice it as best as you can, and it will produce big dividends in your spiritual walk.

STILLNESS AND CONTEMPLATIVE PRAYER

The following practices will help you continue to practice stillness in silence and solitude, and we will then add different forms of contemplative prayer.

"Be still, and know that I am God."—Psalm 46:10a, NIV

"Come to me, all you who are weary and burdened and I will give you rest. Take my yoke upon you and learn from me, for I am gentle and humble in heart, and you will find rest for your souls. For my yoke is easy and my burden is light."—Matthew 11:28–30, NIV

PRACTICING STILLNESS

Begin by practicing stillness, using breathing as the mechanism to quiet yourself. Every time you practice these contemplative disciplines, start by practicing stillness. It is an amazingly restful practice in and of itself. And, it also quiets the mind to prepare it for contemplating God's presence and resting and abiding in his presence.

Get in a quiet place, with no distractions. You will want to also practice the spiritual disciplines of silence and solitude as you engage practicing stillness.

You can practice this sitting, lying down, or walking. This is your choice…whatever supports you being able to focus best. If you are sitting, sit with your back straight and your feet flat on the floor. If you are lying down, lie is a comfortable pose. If you are walking, walk with your head level, back straight, and looking ahead.

- Close your eyes (unless you are walking), and start paying attention to your breathing. Deeply inhale, through your nose, all the way deep into your belly. Your stomach should go out as you inhale. Exhale through your mouth. Focus on your breath as you inhale and as you exhale.

- Calm your mind and release the constant chatter of your mind by attending to your breathing. See your breath go in and out in your mind's eye. Your mind may not want to calm down. You may have difficulty releasing the need to think thoughts. This is all perfectly normal and no problem at all. The important thing is to simply bring your attention back to your breathing when you do notice your mind wandering.

- The two most important attitudes to practice this with are PATIENCE and NON-JUDGMENT. To practice non-judgmentally is to be accepting of whatever is. In other words, even if your mind wanders all the time, you do not judge yourself for not doing it well, you simply notice it, and bring your mind back without resisting that this occurred.

- When you are practicing stillness, you are observing with love—not with resistance, judgment, analysis, or labeling—just observe with love and reverence.

- Turn your attention inward and notice your physical sensations and feelings. Just notice them. Do not feel compelled to do anything about them.

- Do this for at least a few minutes per day. In the beginning, two minutes is a win, and twelve minutes is a home run. Ultimately you will want to expand the time you do this. It is a delightful experience to simply be still and PRACTICE stillness. It sets the stage for a deeper experience of God and yourself.

CONTEMPLATION AND CONTEMPLATIVE PRAYER

After practicing stillness, experiment with the various forms of contemplation I mentioned in this chapter. In addition to the ways we have engaged contemplation and contemplative prayer in previous chapters, there are many other things you can do.

Here are some options you can choose from. Pick one option each day and practice it. But, you are not limited in any way regarding this. If you come up with some ways to practice contemplative prayer that I don't list here, go for it. You get to exercise maximum creativity regarding this.

Some contemplative prayer options to consider:

- Breathe in peace and rest, and breathe out tension, stress, anxiety or worry.

- Breathe in wisdom and breathe out whatever gets in the way of wisdom for you.

- Breathe in God's utter delight in you and breathe out your utter delight in God.

- If you are sick, inhale God's healing power and exhale all sources of the sickness from your body.

- Breathe in the Spirit of God and exhale (releasing) your flawed nature.

- Breathe in God's love and exhale old judgments of others and yourself.

- Inhale God's love and exhale love and kindness to those closest to you and others who come to mind.

- Inhale God's healing power and exhale that healing power toward friends who are sick.

- Inhale gratitude and exhale resentment.

- Inhale gratitude and exhale gratitude to God.

- Play music in the background that settles you and calms you.

- Do this outside in nature.

- Do this while walking in nature.

- All of this is occurring in your mind's eye.

- If you notice tension in your body, follow your breath as it goes into your body to a relaxed area close to the tension, and envision the relaxed area unraveling the tensed area into relaxation as you exhale and inhale again.

- Focus on a picture or work of art that represents God to you. Openly contemplate while attending to breathing and focusing on that picture.

- Hum or chant while contemplating. Sometimes this can help you focus. Or play Gregorian style chanting and singing in the background.

Enjoy experimenting with multiple things from this section and see what resonates with you.

CHAPTER 8

FORGIVENESS: THE FOUNDATION OF FREEDOM

In the magnificent Lord's Prayer, which I also call the Apprentice's Prayer, Jesus addresses forgiveness.

> And forgive us our debts, as we also have forgiven our debtors. (Matthew 6:12, NIV)

It is interesting that the term "debts" is used in this verse. The reality is that when we harm another, or "sin against" them, we owe them a debt tied to the harm done. To forgive another who has harmed you is to give the debt back. It is to release the offense caused and no longer hold the other accountable to owe you.

This ran completely contrary to the Old Testament logic of "an eye for an eye." In that logic, you had the right to expect another to pay a price for harm done to you. Jesus completely reversed that cultural standard.

ENGAGING YOUR VISION

Consider who you have not forgiven in your life. Perhaps you have forgiven them but you still carry hurt, disappointment, or numbness regarding it. That usually is a sign that there is more work to be done. Forgiveness is not a one-off act. Often it is an ongoing practice, every time a particular hurt or offense or betrayal comes to mind.

Just moments before talking about forgiveness during the Sermon on the Mount, Jesus shredded the eye-for-an-eye logic of the day and told his listeners to replace vengeance with mercy and generosity (Matthew 5:38–42).

He then took it a step further in Matthew 5:43–48 by instructing his followers to replace the current standard of the day of loving their neighbor and hating their enemy with loving their enemies and praying for those who persecuted them. It's easy to read this and gloss over it, but the ramifications of actually living this in the day-to-day machinations of life are profound.

THE CENTRALITY OF FORGIVENESS FOR AN APPRENTICE

After his explicit instructions on how to pray in Matthew 6:9–13, Jesus reemphasized one discipline, and one discipline only, to make sure they remembered what was most important about that prayer:

> For if you forgive other people when they sin against you, your heavenly Father will also forgive you. But if you do not forgive others their sins, your Father will not forgive your sins. (Matthew 6:14–15, NIV)

This wasn't just rhetoric. Jesus was introducing a new kingdom-of-heaven reality. He was telling us that the inevitable outcome of extending mercy, generosity, and love is forgiveness. He embodied this from the cross as he prayed for his crucifiers, saying "Father, forgive them, for they know not what they do." He had the capacity and the right to expect justified retribution against his murderers (Matthew 26:53). He was innocent (Matthew 27:4, 19). Yet, he willingly gave up his life to pay the price to restore our full access to God (Romans 3:25, Hebrews 2:17, 1 Corinthians 5:7).

Jesus had every legal right to expect and to extract a just compensation for his suffering and loss. Yet, he forgave. He gave back the debt. And he asks us to do the same (Colossians 3:13).

To not forgive another is to ignore or render irrelevant Jesus's sacrifice.

In Matthew 6, during the Sermon on the Mount, Jesus set the new reality of forgiveness, *and then he lived it.* He laid the foundation for us to embrace forgiveness willingly if we choose.

My pursuit of embracing forgiveness as a genuine reality in my life has come gradually over the years. I think, at first, I gave it lip service—it sounded interesting, but it wasn't meant to be taken seriously in all walks of life. Rather, I would simply apply forgiveness selectively and leave it out of situations where it simply was "not practical."

Expressing contempt at times for those of opposing beliefs, politics, and worldviews, and for those who had wronged me or betrayed me—most of whom were not even sworn enemies exactly—still made a lot of sense to me. After all, *I'm right, and they're wrong,* I reasoned. Or I am only responding to their lies, contempt, and anger.

My reasoning seemed justified. If someone opposed me in a business dispute and was dishonest or injurious in their demeanor and actions, I thought in terms of win-lose. I win, they lose. They needed to learn a lesson and pay. At times these attitudes were subtle and at other times blatant.

Gradually, it started dawning on me that Jesus was expecting me to live *his way.* Perhaps you think this approach impractical in a world where you are constantly interacting with people who do not live by the same credo. Plenty of married folks don't feel compelled at all to apply this in their marriages. The same goes for many of my divorced friends with their former spouses.

Living a life of forgiveness is possible, and when Jesus's teaching is applied, it has the potential to be transformational—not just for the individuals involved, but far beyond that—it can have a multi-generational impact.

Consider what Martin Luther King wrote in his 1963 book, *Strength to Love.* And, I ask you to consider what Dr. King was up against in 1963. He was sailing upwind, to be sure…

> Probably no admonition of Jesus has been more difficult to follow than the command to love your enemies…some have felt that its actual practice is not possible. It is easy, they say, to love those who love you, but how can one love those who openly and insidiously seek to defeat you…?
>
> Far from being the pious injunction of a utopian dreamer, the command to love one's enemy is an absolute necessity for our survival. Love even for our enemies is the key to the solution of the problems of our world. Jesus is not an impractical idealist; he is the practical realist…

Returning hate for hate multiplies hate, adding deeper darkness to a night already devoid of stars. Darkness cannot drive out darkness; only light can do that. Hate cannot drive out hate; only love can do that. Hate multiplies hate, violence multiplies violence, and toughness multiplies toughness in a descending spiral of destruction ...

Love is the only force capable of transforming an enemy into a friend. We never get rid of an enemy by getting rid of enmity. But by its very nature, hate destroys and tears down; by its very nature, love creates and builds up. Love transforms with redemptive power.[31]

It is impossible to fully live love without embracing forgiveness. King and his followers were facing intense hatred from the segregationists. They were not in a position of historical, societal, or political power. They were being actively persecuted. Yet, King goes on:

We must develop and maintain the capacity to forgive. Whoever is devoid of the power to forgive is devoid of the power to love. It is impossible even to begin the act of loving one's enemies without the prior acceptance of the necessity, over and over again, of forgiving those who inflict evil and injury upon us. It is also necessary to realize that the forgiving act must always be initiated by the person who has been wronged, the victim of some great hurt, the recipient of some tortuous injustice, the absorber of some terrible act of oppression. The wrongdoer may request forgiveness. They may come to themselves, and like the prodigal son, move up some dusty road, their heart palpitating with the desire for forgiveness. But only the injured neighbor, the loving father back home, can really pour out the warm waters of forgiveness.

Forgiveness does not mean ignoring what has been done or putting a false label on an evil act. It means, rather, that the evil act no longer remains as a barrier to the relationship. Forgiveness is a catalyst creating the atmosphere necessary for a fresh start and a new beginning...

To our most bitter opponents we say: "We shall match your capacity to inflict suffering by our capacity to endure suffering.

We shall meet your physical force with soul force. Do to us what you will, and we shall continue to love you. We cannot in all good conscience obey your unjust laws, because non-cooperation with evil is as much a moral obligation as is cooperation with good. Throw us in jail, and we shall still owe you. Send your hooded perpetrators of violence into our community at the midnight hour and beat us and leave us half dead, and we shall still love you. But be ye assured that we will wear you down by our capacity to suffer. One day we shall win our freedom, but not only for ourselves, we shall so appeal to your heart and conscience that we shall win you in the process, and our victory will be a double victory."[32]

Martin Luther King Jr. used his commitment to Jesus's challenge in the Sermon on the Mount to change history. The ramifications of his success are far-reaching around the world. He ultimately gave his life for his cause—assassinated by a purveyor of hate. But his example infused the movement he led, and it changed a nation. In America, we are still working out our imperfections. But, we have shining beacons from our history to guide us on what works. And Martin Luther King's words above shine brightly as a beacon.

I ask you to simply consider his example—his inspiration in the midst of extraordinarily difficult times. Consider the impact it made and the transformation it inspired. King's commitment did not end well for him personally. Yet, in God's economy of kingdom-of-heaven living, God had and still has his back eternally. And his stand and dream can still inspire and move people today, all these decades later.

Where in your life, can you embrace Martin Luther King Jr.'s example of forgiveness to forge new possibilities? Don't ignore it. Identify it, and pursue it.

FORGIVENESS AS A LIFESTYLE

In God's economy, Jesus's challenge to forgive, no matter what, is the only logical step to take. It is a mind-set, an attitude of the heart that Jesus instructed his disciples to live in. The point is, if you are committed to being an apprentice of Jesus, this is the standard. If you sow unforgiveness in your relationships in life, it poisons your heart and your ability to walk in the freedom God's forgiveness provides you. *Forgiveness is a fundamental standard for living.*

Perhaps you feel you have handled forgiveness well: that in the areas where it's needed, you've forgiven and continue to forgive. Or perhaps you are clear you have not. Perhaps you are somewhere in between. My request is, no matter how you assess your commitment to forgiveness in your life, give it a completely fresh reconsideration.

My personal point of view is that there are always (and I do mean always) deeper levels of forgiveness possible for every one of us. Not just from a theoretical point of view. From a very practical, pragmatic, work-to-be-done point of view. We never, ever fully plumb the depths of this consideration to such a degree that there is no more work to be done. Forgiveness is not a one-off dynamic. It is a holistic, all-encompassing way of life that Jesus invites us into.

Jesus is explicitly clear that if you desire the extension of another's mercy and forgiveness when you miss the mark, you need to extend the same mercy—whenever it is needed and however many times it is needed. Henri Nouwen says, "Forgiveness is the name of love practiced among people who love poorly. The hard truth is that all people love poorly. We need to forgive and be forgiven every day, every hour increasingly. That is the great work of love among the fellowship of the weak that is the human family."

To claim that I love without embracing forgiveness is a mirage—a grand self-delusion. Forgiveness is at the very heart of love (1 John 2:9).

THE THREEFOLD EMBRACE OF FORGIVENESS

To truly embrace forgiveness in our lives encompasses three different elements: God's forgiveness of us, our forgiveness of others, and finally, the forgiveness we seek from others. We will spend the rest of this chapter looking at each one of these.

I. GOD'S REMISSION AND FORGIVENESS OF YOU MISSING THE MARK

It is impossible to live love outside of a deep embracing of God's forgiveness in your life. First, you get to embrace God's initial and ongoing forgiveness extended toward you as a free gift.

Peter said, "Change your life. Turn to God and be baptized, each of you, in the name of Jesus Christ, so your sins are forgiven. Receive the gift of the Holy Spirit. The promise is targeted to you and your children, but also to all who are far away—whomever, in fact, our Master God invites." (Acts 2:38, MSG)

In the New King James version below, the word translated "forgiven" in *The Message* version above is rendered "remission." This word means that the debt owed is completely wiped out and eliminates all punishment due:

Then Peter said to them, "Repent, and let every one of you be baptized in the name of Jesus Christ for the remission of sins; and you shall receive the gift of the Holy Spirit." (Acts 2:38, NKJV)

Fully embracing this act of mercy from God is a fundamental posture of the heart. It is a hallmark of an apprentice of Jesus. You have been forgiven. Now, it is your turn to forgive others who have harmed you.

In working with people over the years, it has become more and more clear to me how challenging it is for humans to embrace God's forgiveness. If you embrace this, from a practical point of view, you have to release your self-judgments, your beliefs that you do not deserve God's love, that you are not enough, that your mistakes are too large to overcome, that you are not worthy to live and walk in true freedom. This reality of the remission of sins is much easier to accept intellectually than it is to embrace experientially. Yet, not to embrace it is a slap in the face of Jesus's sacrifice for us.

In addition to God's initial remission of our sins and shortcomings with the new birth Peter references in Acts 2:38, we also have the ongoing offer of continued forgiveness—if we do two things.

First, we need to confess our sins—where we miss the mark (1 John 1:9). Own your human imperfection and live in that reality openly with your fellow apprentices. Second, we need to forgive others, as Jesus stated. To not forgive others is to forsake love. And to forsake love takes us completely outside the dynamics of God's community of transformative love.

With the new birth, God wipes the slate clean for us. From then on, in gratitude, we get to practice extending his mercy and forgiveness toward others, which keeps us within the context of his will and forgiveness toward us. That is the moment-by-moment choice continually before us.

I think the concept of "forgiving yourself" falls within the reality of embracing God's ongoing love for us via *his* extension of forgiveness and mercy toward us. His mercy is his withholding of merited judgment. His forgiveness is the act of extending his mercy to us. It is the deepest level of acceptance possible. It is to be *beloved*. This mercy and forgiveness are the sum of the entire gospel. And to embrace them is to step into the warmth of God's embrace, to be surrounded by it, to relax into it, to befriend it, to rest in it. It is to allow it to seep into the pores of your soul and the deepest crevices of your heart. It is to fully embrace it, to embody it, not to recoil from its brilliance but to stand naked before it and in it, with no shame, in complete surrender to its grace. It is to recognize his indwelling presence within.

2. FORGIVING OTHERS

The second aspect of embracing forgiveness is to forgive others, giving to others what you have received.

That sounds simple on the surface, doesn't it? And in one respect, it is. Forgiveness is a choice to give back the debt owed by the offender, the one who harmed you. The one who disappointed you, betrayed you, abandoned you, rejected you, lied to you—whatever it is—forgiveness is the decision to release it.

Sometimes it can be challenging to recognize where we might still hold unforgiveness in our hearts. This is especially true related to past hurts where we already have worked on forgiveness. The results of unconscious unforgiveness will often give it away. Pointers might include things like avoiding vulnerability, unwillingness to trust, shame, resentment, judging, and defensiveness. If you notice these or similar attitudes in your interactions and thought life, be curious and consider what their source is that you may not be currently aware of.

I'll never forget a conversation I had with Katie, my wife, in March of 1996. We were in the middle of a workshop that focused on the importance of forgiveness. After the session one evening, Katie said to me, "I think you still have some forgiveness issues for your dad."

I immediately responded with, "No, I don't. I have really worked on that and it is handled." I noticed how much defensive energy I had in my response. That is almost always an indication that there is something there to consider. Katie responded, "Well, will you please just consider it?" I grudgingly responded that I would.

I did consider it—for months. I was working on creating more intimacy in my relationship with my two sons, who were sixteen and thirteen, at that time. It was within the context of my vision for more intimacy with them that I considered forgiveness in relation to my dad. As I reflectively considered what was blocking deeper intimacy with my sons, I started seeing indicators of unforgiveness for my dad in the language I had used in the recent past. One thing I would say to myself was that I was committed to "being the dad my father never was." This was related to his not being there the way I desired after my parents' divorce when I was six.

I came to realize that my stated commitment of how I was going to parent my boys was rooted in residual unforgiveness and the resulting judgment toward my dad. This was still present even though I had done major work on forgiveness for him over the years. No wonder I was sowing a lack of intimacy in my relationship with my boys!

Unforgiveness automatically leads to a resistance to risk with others, and intimacy always looks and feels vulnerable—like a risk. I was unconsciously resisting deeper intimacy with my boys—I was afraid I would fail in the same way I was judging my dad. And in turn, I was creating distance in my relationship with my boys, which was just the thing I had judged my dad for. What you refuse to forgive will work its way into your current relationships. Unforgiveness is a form of resisting the reality of your life. And what we resist, persists.

What you refuse to transform will surely be transmitted to others.

I also came to realize over a period of months that fear of failure and rejection were major factors in the way I related with my boys. I was overly patriarchal, directive, and opinionated. They knew I loved them, but I was not inviting them to deep intimacy. This was driven by my desire to not screw up my parenting with them—a fear of failure. This too was fueled in part by my judgment and unforgiveness of my dad. I didn't want to screw it up like I judged him to have done. I was afraid I would lose what I had with my sons if I risked deeper intimacy and the vulnerability I unconsciously sensed that would require. What if I was honest with them about my fears and where I struggled? Would they still love me? Would they still respect and appreciate me?

As a result of my new awareness, I started opening up more with my boys about what was going on for me, and I started to listen more to what excited them—what they were passionate about. It didn't happen overnight. We just chipped away at it. By being curious about their passions, I started releasing the need for things to be according to my agenda and started listening more closely to the agenda that was being birthed in their hearts. Inquiring about and learning about my older son's love for music reawakened in me a deep appreciation for music and a love of beauty that had been mostly dormant since I graduated from high school. I received much more from these interchanges than I gave. I was surprised by what it stirred within me.

How much I applied this would ebb and flow at times, but I was so relieved that my deeper honesty with them created a new opening for connection rather than disconnection. They appreciated it. All they had wanted all along was to be connected to a more real version of me anyway.

We are still on this path now that they are adults, all these years later. I have dropped the ball and missed the mark many times since then. But my behavioral shift did change the nature of our relationship to one of deeper intimacy. And the starting point for that was my considering afresh what additional work I needed to do to forgive my father. After working at this for several years, I started to feel empathy and compassion for my dad. That led to deeper levels of gratitude for him. That process too is still ongoing, even though he died four years before I started this self-reflective process in 1996.

3. SEEKING FORGIVENESS FROM OTHERS

The third aspect of embracing forgiveness is seeking forgiveness from others. It is not enough to embrace God's forgiveness and to forgive others. In fact, it is impossible to embrace forgiving others unless we recognize our own inescapable need for forgiveness from them for where we fall short. Asking for forgiveness and seeking reconciliation with those we have harmed is a fundamental building block of living, authentic relationship and authentic community.

As we embrace forgiveness in all three ways laid out in this chapter, we clear space for love to work in and through us. Jesus connected forgiveness *for* us and forgiveness *from* us in the Apprentice's Prayer, suggesting that a lifestyle of ongoing forgiveness is essential to an ongoing, conversational, authentic walk with our Father in heaven.

APPRENTICING WITH JESUS THROUGH PRAYER:
WHERE ARE YOU?

Forgiveness, both accepting it for ourselves and extending it to others, requires a bedrock trust in God, expressed in our willingness to be authentic and naked before him. Prayer is where we work this trust out with God.

Why do we resist trusting God in all our vulnerability and nakedness with all our shortcomings on full display and fully acknowledged? Perhaps we feel the same automatic fear of vulnerability, of falling short. Perhaps we feel shame for where we feel unworthy of his goodness—the heritage we have inherited from Adam and Eve.

Author Thomas Keating says in his book, *The Human Condition:*

Where are you? This is one of the great questions of all time. It is the focus of the first half of the spiritual journey.

Biblical scholars and readers will remember that in Genesis 3 it is the question God asked when Adam and Eve had taken off for the underbrush after their disobedience. He called out to them and said, "Adam, where are you?" They were hiding in the woods, and God was looking for them. Adam said, "We heard your voice, and we were scared because we were naked." So God said, "How did you know you were naked?"

This marvelous story of creation is not just about Adam and Eve. It is really about us. It is a revelation of where we are. The same question is addressed to every generation, time and person. At every moment of our lives, God is asking us, "Where are you? Why are you hiding?"

All the questions that are fundamental to human happiness arise when we ask ourselves this excruciating question: Where am I? Where am I in relation to God, to myself, and to others? These are the basic questions of human life.

As soon as we answer honestly, we have begun the spiritual search for God, which is also the search for ourselves. God is asking us to face the reality of the human condition, to come out of the woods into the full light of intimacy with him. That is the state of the mind that Adam and Eve had, according to the story, before their disobedience. As soon as they became aware of their separation from God, they headed for the woods. They had to hide from God because the loss of the intimacy and union that they had enjoyed with him in paradise was so painful.[33]

Jesus reestablished the relationship with God that was lost in the garden of Eden in a fresh, new way (Romans 3:23–26). He has blazed a path for us to stand before God with no shame, guilt, or fear. We have complete freedom to be naked before him—to say, "This is where I am" with no hiding or shame.

Prayer is an ongoing conversation with God rooted in this reality. It embraces it, revels in it, is humbled by it, and honors it. It celebrates and delights in it. It stands naked in its light, rather than hiding in the shadows of shame, avoidance, minimization and rationalization.

STILLNESS AND CONTEMPLATING FORGIVENESS

We will continue to practice stillness in silence and solitude, and then practice contemplating forgiveness.

"Be still, and know that I am God."—Psalm 46:10a

"Then Peter came to Jesus and asked, 'Lord, how many times shall I forgive my brother or sister who sins against me? Up to seven times?' Jesus answered, 'I tell you, not seven times, but seventy-seven times.'"—Matthew 18:21-22, NIV

PRACTICING STILLNESS

Start by practicing stillness, using breathing as the mechanism to quiet yourself. Every time you practice these contemplative disciplines, you start with practicing stillness. It is an amazingly restful practice in and of itself. And, it also quiets the mind to prepare it for contemplating God's presence and resting and abiding in his presence.

Get in a quiet place with no distractions. You will want to also practice the spiritual disciplines of silence and solitude as you engage practicing stillness.

You can practice this sitting, laying down, or walking...whatever supports you being able to focus best. If you are sitting, sit with your back straight and your feet flat on the floor. If you are lying down, lie is a comfortable pose. If you are walking, walk with your head level, back straight and looking ahead.

- (Unless you are walking) Close your eyes, and start paying attention to your breathing. Deeply inhale, through your nose, all the way deep into your belly. Your stomach should go out as you inhale. Exhale through your mouth. Focus on your breath as you inhale and as you exhale.

- Calm your mind and release the constant chatter of your mind by attending to your breathing. See your breath go in and out in your mind's eye. Your mind may not want to calm down. You may have difficulty releasing the need to think thoughts. This is all perfectly normal and no problem at all. The important thing is to simply bring your attention back to your breathing when you do notice your mind wandering.

- The two most important attitudes to practice this with are PATIENCE and NON-JUDGMENT. To practice non-judgmentally is to be accepting of whatever is. In other words, even if your mind wanders all the time, you do not judge yourself for not doing it well, you simply notice it, and bring your mind back without resisting that this occurred.

- When you are practicing stillness, you are observing with love—not with resistance, judgment, analysis, or labeling—just observation with love and reverence.

- Turn your attention inward and notice your physical sensations and feelings. Just notice them. Do not feel compelled to do anything about them.

- Do this for at least a few minutes per day. In the beginning, two minutes is a win, and twelve minutes is a home run. Ultimately you will want to expand the time you do this. It is a delightful experience to simply be still and PRACTICE stillness. It sets the stage for a deeper experience of God and yourself.

CONTEMPLATING FORGIVENESS

Now, you have an opportunity to do some deep work regarding forgiveness. First, consider your vision you have declared for your time in this study. Is any aspect of this vision hindered by existing hurt, disappointment, pain, suffering, or betrayal caused by another? If you are not sure or if you think your answer to that question is "no," I still encourage you to stay open to it as a possibility.

We so often bury hurts from long ago in our unconsciousness, but they leave wounds that are not healed. And often we excuse or minimize the actions of another as a means to distance ourselves from the pain we feel. So, I am asking you to be open to what may be there but that you are not currently considering.

Identifying this is an opportunity to practice giving back the debt of the offense they caused. You can do this contemplatively and prayer without words is especially effective with this.

And, you may have people who readily come to mind that you know you have forgiveness work to do.

If you are struggling to genuinely embrace forgiveness for them, consider this:

- Holding on to unforgiveness is like drinking poison yourself, hoping the other will die.

- The pain of unforgiveness that you currently feel will either be transformed by your embracing of forgiveness or the pain will surely be transmitted to others.

This is a very simple contemplative exercise.

- Bring the person to mind, clear your mind of extraneous thoughts, notice your internal state—your emotions and physical sensations. If you are upset, allow God to comfort you in that moment. Rest in him.

- Inhale God's forgiveness for you—his unconditional love, mercy and forgiveness for you despite all the times you have fallen short. Inhale it deeply into every cell of your body.

- Exhale your forgiveness for the person you have in mind. See them in your mind's eye and exhale forgiveness towards them. It is okay if it is difficult for you and if you notice resistance to doing it. Simply practice it. Release any resistance you feel to the best of your ability. Just release it all into God's arms.

- Then inhale your gratitude for God's mercy that he has forgiven you. Deeply inhale his mercy and grace—you are completely forgiven and whole in his eyes.

- Then exhale God's mercy and grace towards your designated person. See them through God's eyes. Practice it.

Continue alternating these areas of contemplation for the duration of the time you have allocated to do this. You can do this every day with one person, or alternate with different people you see you need to engage forgiveness for at a deeper level. Practice this every day.

CHAPTER 9

PEACE AND GRATITUDE

We live in an age of anxiety in one of the most stressed-out countries in the world:

- Three quarters of Americans experience physical and psychological symptoms related to stress in a given month.
- One third report living with extreme stress.
- Half believe their stress has increased over the last five years.
- Half of Americans report lying awake at night due to stress.[34]
- Workplace stress costs more than $300 billion per year in health care, missed work, and stress-reduction costs.[35]

Anxiety disorders are the most common type of mental illness in the US, affecting 40 million adults and costing more than $42 billion per year in care costs. People with anxiety disorders are three to five times more likely to go to a doctor and six times more likely to be hospitalized for psychiatric disorders.[36] Women are twice as likely to be affected as men.[37]

ENGAGING YOUR VISION

Think of the specifics of your vision you declared for your time in this *Apprenticing Jesus* study. Think in terms of gratitude relative to the challenges you have experienced. Where do you notice that embracing gratitude can propel you forward?

And all these statistics are only referring to *professionally diagnosed* people. They do not include all the people who have not been diagnosed but still suffer from anxiety, stress, and worry. Thirty-nine percent of

Millennials say their stress is increasing.[38] People indicate their top stressors are money (69 percent), work (65 percent), and the economy (61 percent).[39]

The antidote for worry, stress, and anxiety is *peace*. Jesus had a lot to say about it. In this chapter, we will explore what it means to live in peace—and its natural correlation, gratitude.

THE ANTIDOTE

In the Sermon on the Mount, Jesus addressed our stress and offered an antidote:

> Therefore I tell you, do not worry about your life, what you will eat or drink; or about your body, what you will wear. Is not life more than food, and the body more than clothes? Look at the birds of the air; they do not sow or reap or store away in barns, and yet your heavenly Father feeds them. Are you not much more valuable than they? Can any one of you by worrying add a single hour to your life?
>
> And why do you worry about clothes? See how the flowers of the field grow. They do not labor or spin. Yet I tell you that not even Solomon in all his splendor was dressed like one of these. If that is how God clothes the grass of the field, which is here today and tomorrow is thrown into the fire, will he not much more clothe you—you of little faith? So do not worry, saying, "What shall we eat?" or "What shall we drink?" or "What shall we wear?" For the pagans run after all these things, and your heavenly Father knows that you need them.
>
> But seek first his kingdom and his righteousness, and all these things will be given to you as well. Therefore do not worry about tomorrow, for tomorrow will worry about itself. Each day has enough trouble of its own. (Matthew 6:25-34, NIV)

Verse 30 gives a key path to overcoming worry and anxiety: faith.

Faith is beautifully defined in Hebrews 11:1, KJV: "Now faith is the substance of things hoped for, the evidence of things not seen." Faith generates peace. So how do we get to the point where we more fully embrace faith rather than worry, anxiety, and stress?

Colossians 3 has a treasure trove of insights regarding creating peace in our lives:

> Let the peace of Christ rule in your hearts, since as members of one body you were called to peace. And be thankful. Let the message of Christ dwell among you richly as you teach and admonish one another with all wisdom through psalms, hymns, and songs from the Spirit, singing to God with gratitude in your hearts. And whatever you do, whether in word or deed, do it all in the name of the Lord Jesus, giving thanks to God the Father through him. (Colossians 3:15–17, NIV)

In verse 15 we are encouraged to let the peace of God *rule* in our hearts—and to be thankful. We'll get to that second part in a moment, but first, this word "rule" is interesting. It means to act as an umpire in the public games and to be enthroned as decider of everything.[40] The word "peace" in this verse means to be free from anxiety and denotes the absence of strife. It denotes a state of untroubled, undisturbed well-being.

Faith is the foundation of this way of being. Faith is trusting that God will be with us—always, no matter what—even when life makes no sense and we suffer loss, disappointment, betrayal, or tragedy. The only way we can trust in this way is to see life in the present as a current expression of living eternally—now and into the future, including when this life is over. Our trust in God needs to be contextualized within his perspective of eternity, not merely here in this flawed world. He promises he will never leave us or forsake us (Hebrews 13:6, Psalm 118:6). He is a redemptive God. He takes the tragedies and betrayals of life and redeems them—if not fully in this life, then in the next.

If we are willing to let the peace of God rule in our hearts and embrace gratitude, these things will open up an entirely new way of relating to all the challenges of life. Walking in this way is utterly transformational.

The Colossians passage tells us that freedom from anxiety and strife and an untroubled, undisturbed well-being can be preeminent in our life. All fears of not being enough and not having enough are replaced with trust in the acceptance and abundance of God.

135

THE KEY TO GRATITUDE

Immediately following the exhortation to let the peace of Christ rule in our hearts, we are encouraged to "be thankful." The word for "thankful" in this verse is also often translated *grateful* or *gratitude*. Verse 16 tells us that the predominant attitude to embrace as we connect and interact in God's family is "gratitude in our hearts." We are told in verse 17 that whatever we do is to be done while "giving thanks to God." Again, this word "thanks" is interchangeably translated *thanks* and *gratitude*.

The context of Colossians 3:15 is the posture of our hearts. The heart is the center of our being. Infusing our hearts with gratitude is foundational to living in peace. Gratitude generates faith that generates peace.

The context of verse 16 is our interactions with each other in God's family. The passage again instructs us to do this with "gratitude in our hearts" as we sing to God. Gratefulness to God should be the foundational attitude in our interactions with each other. Think about what your predominant attitudes are when interacting with others. God encourages us to have gratitude as the foundation.

Verse 17 expands the scope to "whatever you do," giving thanks to God—being grateful.

Look at the progression of the expansion of gratitude in our lives that is detailed here:

- First, let the posture of your heart be full of gratitude. Become aware and pay attention to your inner being.

- Second, let all interactions with others in God's family be done with gratitude. Pay attention to those committed to walking out the love of God together with you, and be grateful for them and with them.

- Third, let everything you do be based in gratitude. Be a walking, talking everywhere-you-go expression of gratitude. Bring it to the world.

PUTTING IT INTO PRACTICE

How do we put Colossians 3:15–17 into practice? First, pay attention to the posture of your heart. Notice if anxiety, worry, or conflict (judgment, annoyances, offenses) are present. If so, release them and choose to embrace gratitude.

Next, practice living out that gratitude with your fellow apprentices in God's glorious, transformative community of love. One of the great purposes of being a part of the family of God—the "body of Christ"—is to practice love. Gratitude is an essential part of that.

Then, take the momentum you are building in embracing gratitude in your personal focused silence, solitude, and prayer with God and use it to ground your interactions with your fellow apprentices in gratitude. Then expand it to your entire sphere of influence. Let your "kingdom"—the entirety of your sphere of influence—be a living expression of gratitude.

THE INTERPLAY OF FAITH AND ANXIETY

Embracing gratitude is the most effective practice that supports releasing worry and anxiety and replacing them with peace. It also generates faith, the pathway to peace. Earlier in this chapter, we looked at Jesus's instructions regarding overcoming worry and anxiety in the Sermon on the Mount. He said having "little faith" was a cause of worry and anxiety (Matthew 6:30).

Jesus used this phrase "you of little faith" five times in the Gospels. These fascinating references show the four key mind-sets that diminish faith. First, in Matthew 6:30 and in Luke 12:28, he illustrates how diminished faith leads to anxiety. In Matthew 8:2, 6 he indicates that diminished faith leads to fear. In Matthew 14:31 he shows that diminished faith leads to doubt. And in Matthew 16:8 he tells us that diminished faith leads to forgetfulness.

You could also flip this and say that forgetfulness, doubt, fear, and anxiety diminish faith. When they occupy space in our hearts, faith cannot coexist with them. When faith occupies space in our hearts, forgetfulness (of what God has done for us), doubt (of what he can do), fear (that he will not be with us and see us through), and anxiety (worrying that he will not deliver us from evil) cannot coexist with it.

Gratitude is a prime ingredient in faith and peace. Let's explore further how to embrace it.

GRATITUDE AS A LIFESTYLE

For gratitude to work, you must identify the barriers to gratitude and develop practical strategies to overcome those barriers. In our culture today, gratitude is in short supply—but we can grow it and cultivate a grateful disposition.

In *Gratitude Works!*, Robert Emmons writes:

> In modern times gratitude has become untethered from its moral moorings, and collectively we are worse off because of this. When the ancient Roman philosopher Cicero stated that gratitude was the queen of the virtues, he most assuredly did not mean that gratitude was merely a stepping stone toward personal happiness. Gratitude is a morally complex disposition, and reducing this virtue to a technique or strategy to improve one's mood is to do it an injustice.
>
> Even restricting gratitude to an inner feeling is insufficient. In the history of ideas, gratitude is considered an action (returning a favor) that is not only virtuous in and of itself but also valuable to society. To reciprocate is the right thing to do ... Conversely, across time, ingratitude has been treated as a serious vice, a greater vice than gratitude is a virtue. Ingratitude is the "essence of vileness," wrote the great German philosopher Immanuel Kant, and David Hume opined that ingratitude is "the most horrible and unnatural crime that a person is capable of committing."[41]

Gratitude is a practice, not an attitude. Practicing it can clearly impact your attitude. But it is built through intentional practices, not whims or in-the-moment feelings.

Some powerful gratitude practices include reflective thinking, journaling, letter writing and gratitude visits—all focused on gratitude and what you are grateful for. The heart of all these practices is memory. Gratitude is about remembering. In order to be grateful, we must remember to remember.[42]

Developing this strength in your life has significant ramifications. Research has shown that gratitude has one of the strongest links to mental health and life satisfaction of any personality trait—more so than even optimism, hope, or compassion. Grateful people experience higher levels of positive emotions such as joy, enthusiasm, love, happiness, and optimism. Also, gratitude as a discipline protects us from the destructive impulses of envy, resentment, greed, and bitterness. It reduces stress and increases overall health.

GRATITUDE AND SPIRITUAL DISCIPLINES

Gratitude is also strengthened with several spiritual disciplines we have not covered in this study: celebration (delighting in each other), fasting (a deeply held sense of gratefulness toward life requires some degree of deprivation[43]), worship (delighting in gratitude to God), and simplicity (not being captured by materialism). These spiritual disciplines, along with silence, solitude, practicing stillness, contemplation, contemplative prayer, and other forms of prayer, are all about connection in relationships—relationship with God, ourselves and each other. And they are all designed to ultimately allow us to experience God most deeply within the community we have with each other.

ENTITLEMENT AND GRATITUDE

The single greatest obstacle to gratitude is an inflated view of self. Self-importance, arrogance, vanity, and a consistent desire to seek approval and admiration all lead to ungratefulness. Humility is fuel for gratefulness (Colossians 3:12). When we become preoccupied with ourselves, we forget and ignore the blessings we receive from others and from God.

The expression of this narcissistic, self-absorbed approach to life, which is rampant in our culture today, is called *entitlement*. Put simply, entitlement means "you owe me." Or "life owes me." Or "I deserve this because life has done me wrong." Entitlement is born from resentment and bitterness, and it breeds envy. It revels in getting its own way, even if it comes at the expense of another. It breeds contempt. It lives in comparison and actively seeks to diminish others in order to enhance itself. At the every least, it is indifferent to the sacrifice of another on its behalf as long as it gets what it thinks it deserves.

Entitlement is jet fuel for adopting a victim mindset. Many people are victimized in life, or harmed by others. But there is a huge difference between being victimized and then living life from the mindset of being a victim. The reverse is also true. Victimhood is also fuel for entitlement. They are joined at the hip. They are fuel for each other. And this mindset is more prevelant in our culture than ever. This mindset is the most toxic mindset I know. It adds nothing of value. And it destroys everything of value if left to runs its course of retribution, vengeance, bitterness, and destruction.

A victim mindset leads to resentment, which breeds bitterness, which births entitlement. And entitlement justifies all sorts of bad behavior rooted in vengeance or revenge.

Entitlement is so pervasive in our culture that it can permeate our perspective in subtle ways. Often we have our own view of what we expect God to do for us rather than being clear on what he has actually promised. He promises to be with us and to comfort us in tribulation (2 Corinthians 1:4). But he does tell us we will experience tribulation and that we are to be patient when it comes (Romans 5:2–4, Romans 12:12). This word "tribulation" means pressure from evils, affliction, and distress.[44] God does not promise a challenge-free life. To expect that is entitled thinking.

Entitlement is a deadly poison, not only for the individual, but for all those around you. It kills gratitude dead in its tracks. And entitlement has infiltrated every political persuasion, religious orientation, and racial group. (Of course, we tend to be clear about how entitlement runs amuck in other people groups while being blind to how it works in us.)

Here is the acid test for determining how much entitlement dwells in your heart at any given moment. How grateful are you? How at peace are you with your current reality in life? How much do you live in complaint? How much do you blame others? How much resentment do you hold and against who?

140

The language of entitlement is complaint and demand. If you notice complaints and implicit and explicit demands or expectations in your life, then gratitude and peace are not ruling in you. Ask yourself, "What do I think I deserve (in life and in relationships) that I'm not getting right now?" That inquiry will ultimately uncover entitlement attitudes and assumptions in yourself that you may not have noticed being present.

I have a request of you. Stop right now and consider how much you are pesonally contextualizing what I am saying in this chapeter right now. Are you saying "I wish so-and-so could read this so they can get their act together and not be so off base in their protestations of victimhood and what they deserve by being victimized." If you are thinking that, think again. You control only one mindset in the universe. That is yours. I know the world is full of people looking to create reactivity in other's response to the events of life so they can influence their actions. And, most people are more than willing to buy into that influence. But, I am asking you to go a different path. Buy into you being a part of God's kingdom, Jesus's apprenticeship plan, and embrace that path.

Be willing to own your own life and your influence. Be committed to make a mark in the world that aligns with Jesus's example of love and courage. And relentlessly interrupt your attitudes that invite you into judging others and making them pay because they do not agree with you.

Instead, be a relentless stand for goodness, patience, courage, action and refuse to capitulate to those attempting to guilt you into cowardice and instead be a stand for gratitude, collaboration, and freedom.

RESISTANCE AND SURRENDER

Entitlement is one of the many ways we resist what is in our lives. We react and resist due to life not showing up the way we think it should. Entitlement is a resistance mindset. And resistance blocks gratitude.

The good news is that resistance is dissolved through acceptance—or surrender. Acceptance clears the stage for gratitude. When confronted with irritations and the inevitable difficulties of life, you can prepare your heart for gratitude to take the stage by practicing surrender and presence.

To surrender means to accept. Acceptance does not mean you are capitulating, condoning, or agreeing. It means to be present with what is rather than resisting it or judging it, even when it is the last thing you prefer or want. Acceptance and surrender are not the same things as "tolerating" or "settling for." They are a different mind-set—a different way of being.

Being present means you are not living in the past—being driven by hauntings, past experiences, or historical assumptions, fears, beliefs, or nostalgia. Being present also means you are not in the future, imagining or anticipating what is next or what could happen or what you are going to do or what or where you would prefer to be.

Presence engages the discipline of embracing current reality as a resource rather than as a problem, like we talked about in a previous chapter. The spiritual disciplines of silence, solitude, stillness, contemplation, and contemplative prayer help birth a more consistent intentionality in being present in the moment.

For example, imagine that your spouse or closest friend becomes positioned and angry in a conversation with you. You could respond by reacting defensively or staying quiet while resenting the way they are behaving, or by being entitled about them showing up in a way you don't deserve. Or you can choose to surrender to the fact that they are upset without feeling the need to condone, capitulate, agree, tolerate, settle, or fix it.

You can choose to remain openhearted in that moment—being curious as to what is happening for them rather than dismissive. You can choose to interpret their anger and rigidity as expressions of some way in which they are suffering because life is not showing up the way they want. No doubt staying surrendered and present in this way requires discipline and interrupting your own tendency to react in kind or take offense. It is challenging. But it is always an option.

Being present with what is, without resisting and judging, enables you to open the eyes of your heart and mind. You now have the possibility of noticing what you were blinded to in your resistance. It is a path to effective action rather than getting stuck in a hostile reaction.

When we jettison resistance in this way, it actually creates an opening for gratitude. This gratitude can take many forms:

- Appreciation for the fact that the other is up against it and gratitude that God promises to be with both of you in this event.

- Gratitude for not allowing yourself to get caught up in reactivity and escalating the upset and breakdown.

- Appreciation for the fact that the other is hurting, and gratefulness to be able to be with them in that moment.

- Remembering that God has extended you mercy in similar circumstances.

- Gratitude for the discovery this difficult conversation is going to lead you into.

It is an opportunity to discover something about the other in that moment that you weren't aware of. You may not make any progress with the other person in reaching agreement about whatever the difference is. But, you will have an entirely different experience in the disagreement if you embrace the attitudes mentioned above. You can disagree and still be calm, open and curious. Or you may find points of agreement. Either way, the way you show up in these kinds of difficult conversations will be a signficant part of the legacy that interaction will generate.

There are lots of ways to engage gratitude in such a moment. This is not an expression of denial. You can be sad with others while being grateful. You can be sad about a breakdown but grateful to be able to walk through it with the other person to deeper connection. If you engage this discipline of staying present, it will generate peace in you in the moment instead of anxiety and stress.

Gratitude requires and enhances openness in mind, heart, and being. We can literally be grateful for everything. This is walking in faith. Gratitude is the key to experiencing joy in the midst of suffering. When someone is caught up in fixations, compulsions, fears, and defense mechanisms, in reality that person is expressing suffering. The suffering is born from an subconscious desperation that life is not going to turn out the way they want in that moment.

Joy is not the absence of suffering or the aftermath of suffering well. There is no linear progression from suffering to joy. Joy involves inviting God's redemptive presence and peace into the suffering.

Gratitude leads to a deeper awareness of the constant presence of grace in our lives—God's divine, unmerited favor. Maintaining an awareness of the constancy of God's presence every moment gives us the courage to be present ourselves rather than escaping into hauntings or imaginations. This is resistance-free living. It is a choice, moment by moment.

One very simple but profoundly powerful practice that can help you stay present in difficult conversations is to attend to your breathing. When you feel yourself getting caught up in reactivity or defensiveness, stop, intentionally deepen your breathing, relax, and ground yourself in being present and neutral. Practicing this in your stillness and contemplation time predisposes you to be able to more effectively remember and do it in the midst of charged and difficult interchanges.

PRACTICING PEACE AND GRATITUDE

We face the challenge of living in an age of anxiety and entitlement, in a culture dominated by these attitudes. Entitlement and anxiety are the "water we swim in," culturally speaking. That is why it is so critical for us to *practice gratitude*. It is something you can always do, if you choose, and it leads to peace ruling your heart and faith determining your orientation in life. In our prayer and contemplative life, gratitude can take a central place. There is always room to express gratitude as you pray. Journaling, which can be a form of written contemplation or prayer, is another way to practice gratitude as a regular part of our daily prayer time.

KEYS TO GRATITUDE JOURNALING

Gratitude journaling is probably the most important gratitude-building practice you can develop as a habit. We will give it a try in our contemplation topics at the end of this chapter.

Several keys to remembering and expressing gratitude through journaling greatly increase its effectiveness and your ability to stick with this practice with enthusiasm. We'll look at three: specificity, surprise, and scarcity.

SPECIFICITY

You probably have heard the statement, "The devil is in the details." Well, the *truth* is also in the details. When you notice an event or action that you are grateful for, when you journal about it, and recall it in detail and get very specific, you will see the beauty and significance of its blessing—even when it is a seemingly small thing.

For example, one recent winter I visited a friend in Connecticut to work on a project together for a few days. This particular winter had been brutally harsh in the Northeast, and they were tiring of the endless stream of snowstorms and unseasonably bitter cold they were experiencing. I flew into Boston and drove the two hours to the Hartford area of Connecticut. On the day I was departing to go back home, we received a foot of snow. It was quite a mess. However, I was able to get out, and I drove through the last remnants of snow to Boston, where I stayed at a hotel near the airport to be ready for a very early-morning flight out the next day.

I can be fairly vague as I remember this incident, or I can be specific and detailed. Each approach will generate a different experience as I recall it. The more specific and detailed my memory, the more the memory will access the emotional part of my brain and evoke a full remembrance that has some punch to it in terms of creating an experience of gratitude.

For example, I could journal that I'm grateful I made it to the airport and that my flight made it out the next day, and that we were able to free my rental car from the foot of snow in my friend's driveway so I could drive to the Boston airport. That would be good and generate some value.

Or I could remember the details of the event, looping in the acts of others that made a difference along the way. For example, here is another remembrance of what happened: I woke up the day of my departure—expecting to leave late that afternoon to go to the hotel near the Boston airport—and found several inches of snow on the ground with the snow still coming down heavy and hard. It looked like I might not be able to leave after all.

However, it quit snowing by noon, thus creating a window in which I could still possibly make it to the airport that night. We would have several hours of shoveling snow ahead of us if we were to secure a path for my car out of the driveway to get to the road. However, my friend called a snowplow contractor who plowed her driveway sometimes and asked them to come do her driveway first. Even though they had other customers who were more regular, they came.

The snow was very wet and heavy—very difficult to plow or shovel. Yet, the two workmen with the contractor got out of the truck and hand-shoveled all the areas the plow was not able to completely clear. They helped me get the snow off my rental car and then get it out of the driveway so they could plow the area where it had been parked. Then they hand-shoveled the entire sidewalk to the front door. They were cheerful and gracious, even though they had a twenty-four-hour workday ahead of them.

By the time I was prepared to leave later that afternoon, all the roads, including the small side roads in the Connecticut town where I was, had been plowed out. I have always been amazed at the remarkable efficiency of most cities and towns in snowy northern climates to remove heavy snowfalls almost by the time the snow has stopped. Due to all the planning, preparation, ready-to-use equipment, and efforts of the employees operating the equipment, there was hardly a hiccup in my original plans.

As I drove along I-84 in Connecticut and then I-90 in Massachusetts, snow was still spitting from the sky, but the roadways were clear of snow and ice due to the heavy snow already having been removed. The roadways had been thoroughly salted, so the smaller amounts of snow were melting as they hit the pavement. Again, the excellence of the snow-removal efforts of both states, including all the manpower, preparation, and tax money allocation for adequate supplies, carried the day. I usually take all of this for granted. But remembering in detail creates an entirely new mind-set.

146

Arriving at the airport late that night, I dropped off my rental car at the airport rental car center and then picked up a shuttle at the airport for the hotel where I was staying. It was bitter cold, but the hotel shuttle arrived promptly. The driver was friendly and knew all the backroads to the hotel to shorten the trip. If you have ever been in Boston, you know how incredibly confusing the roadways there can be. The next morning, the same driver drove the shuttle back to the airport. Even though he had been up all night, he was chipper, alert, and cheerful.

My flight left on time, even though they had to de-ice the plane before departing, and I arrived home safe and sound.

I could go into even more detail if I chose. And I have been on plenty of trips where things did not go as smoothly! Yet, if I choose to recognize and remember them, there are still many, many things to be grateful for on even the most difficult trips.

I often marvel at the undeserved blessing of what I call "the accident of birth" of being born in a country like the United States, where we get to experience an unprecedented level of freedom and opportunity. Even with all the challenges we have today as a country, this blessing still holds true. I had absolutely nothing to do with it. Yet I reap its benefits every single day of my life. I am reaping the collective efforts of literally millions of people who came before me and created what we have today in the US.

Being specific helps us avoid gratitude fatigue. The details are what make the difference and create the emotional resonance of our re-membering. And specificity encourages us to appreciate the giver's efforts. When it comes to gratitude, the truth is in the details. Depth of detail matters.

Assumption plays a big part in missing detail. If I assume that every-thing should go my way, when it does, I miss all sorts of detail because of my assumption that it was supposed to go that way anyway. If I assume things are not going to go my way, then I ignore much of the detail that indicates otherwise, due to my assumption. Once we make an *a priori* decision about how something is supposed to be, the brain actually starts looking for evidence to support that decision so we can feel good about it. The "feel-good" hormone, oxytocin, is actually released by the decision we make about how something is. We unconsciously desire to find additional evidence that our assumption is correct because we crave more of the good feeling an additional release of oxytocin will give us. This can be helpful in that it motivates us to make decisions, take action, and move ahead in life. But when our decision is inaccurate, it can lead to our not noticing evidence to the contrary. This confirmation bias can be a two edged sword.

However, if our decision is to live in gratitude, this feel-good brain dynamic can work in our favor. Gratitude affirms goodness in your life and helps you recognize that the sources of the goodness come at least partially outside yourself.[45]

SURPRISE

Surprise is another aspect of how assumptions can increase or diminish gratitude. Research has shown that surprise is one of the primary drivers of emotional intensity. This is true both for positive emotions (e.g. when receiving an unexpected gift) and negative emotions (e.g. being shocked by an accident). When we feel entitled and expect things we prefer to happen "because we deserve them," we are not surprised when good things *do* happen, and as a result, are less grateful.

If we come from the place of believing everything is a blessing—not something we are automatically entitled to we—will be consistently surprised at the blessings that come our way and experience a deeper emotional experience of gratitude. Keep this in mind as you journal your gratitude.

SCARCITY

When things are going well, we have a tendency to think it is never going to end. However, that is rarely the case. When we are in that mind-set, and things-going-well does end, we hit the inevitable valleys of life. We are surprised, thus intensifying the negative emotions related to the downturn in fortunes. And we miss out on the experience of gratitude when things are going well because we take it for granted that they will.

It is a healthy practice to realize that the good things in your life are not promised forever and could end. Don't assume they will go on forever. It is even valuable to imagine them ending. How would you approach a valued friendship if you knew that person would be leaving soon? How would you treat the important relationships in your life if you knew they (or you) were going to die in the near future? Think about it. The realization of scarcity puts the entire relationship in a different light. You might not get as annoyed with small inconveniences. You might not belabor the common irritations that come in any relationship. You would focus on the gift that person is and the blessing he or she is to you.

The fact is that we all die. And situations come up that change the nature of relationships. Every blessing I have in my life right now will change. It will evolve. And eventually, I will die. I believe God will be with me in that, as he shepherds me to what is next after this life. *But that does not change the immense loss death represents in this life.* Recognizing the reality of scarcity is a powerful motivation to quit majoring in the minors and embrace gratitude for the blessings in your life. All we have is right now. We can't guarantee the future.

The following statement from John Hanley, Sr. beautifully sums up the reality of opportunities passing in life, moment by moment. Please read and consider this in light of the reality of the life we have been given now, here on earth. I know God has promised us a life beyond this. But the desire to embrace *this life* and extend it has been woven into our DNA by God. Realizing the precious gift that life is, and living in gratitude for it, is what matters.

You are entitled to one life and one life only, including one birth and one death. This life is not transferrable. By accepting life, you acknowledge that your participation throughout the course of life and the results you produce are solely your responsibility.

If you exit life early, you may not return. This restriction includes all conditions of premature termination, regardless of cause. There are no do-overs. Neither the length of life nor the quality of life is guaranteed. There are no assurances or warranties. There are no refunds or exchanges. This is it. Enjoy yourself.

GRATITUDE CONTEMPLATION AND JOURNALING

In this section of practices, our focus will be on practicing gratitude-based contemplation and gratitude journaling. We have five contemplation topics in this section. Please be aware that there are additional gratitude-building practices that are powerful, such as gratitude letters (writing a letter to a person who positively impacted your life, expressing your appreciation in detail), and gratitude visits (visiting people who have positively impacted you in your life to express your appreciation in person). But for now, we will focus on gratitude contemplation and gratitude journaling.

Start your quiet time with practicing stillness, as outlined in all the previous chapters. Then, move on to our gratitude practices as outlined below.

As part of embracing gratitude as a practice at the end of each day, I encourage you to write down three things you are grateful for. Write them down in a gratitude journal. Continue this practice for at least thirty days, and then consider what impact it has had on your life over those past thirty days. This is a powerful habit to develop ongoingly.

And enjoy. Practicing gratitude enhances and deepens our joy and delight. It does not avoid suffering but rather acknowledges the inevitability of it, and in doing so, it finds the redemptive imprint of God in even the worst of situations.

In reality, deep gratitude is not possible without embracing the reality of suffering and pain. It is in the surrender to their inevitability that we create space to see the emerging hand of God and the love of others in even the darkest moments of our lives. These gifts are the beacon of light that guides our path forward as we navigate the inevitable challenges of life. That is why noticing and remembering the blessings of God and others is such a critical discipline in life as an apprentice of Jesus.

CONTEMPLATION TOPIC 1:
JOURNALING GRATEFULNESS

After you engage your silence, solitude, stillness, and contemplation time, start a gratitude journal. I keep my gratitude journal in my iPhone Notes because I always have that with me. Whatever device you use for your journal—a handwritten notebook, an electronic device, etc.—it is helpful to use something you always have with you so that you can journal about what you are grateful for whenever it comes to mind.

Plan on adding to your gratitude journal several times per week. Always date your entries. You can make this a lifelong habit and keep your journal as a reminder of God's goodness in your life, through his direct gifts and through the gifts given through others.

CONTEMPLATION FOCUS

Contemplate the scripture from Romans below with gratitude.

In your journal, start by considering what you are grateful for right now. Think of anything that occurs to you, and write about it. If you can, spend at least ten minutes writing. If you don't have ten minutes, go ahead and spend as much time as you have. Even two minutes of writing about someone you appreciate with specificity is a good start. At a minimum, add three more things you are grateful for.

Remember to:

- Be specific and detailed in your remembrance of blessings from others that come to mind.

- Consider things that surprised you that you are grateful for.

- Consider the temporal nature of the blessings you received—the reality that they could go away. Be thankful for them in light of that.

And we know that in all things God works for the good of those who love him, who have been called according to his purpose ... in all these things we are more than conquerors through him who loved us. For I am convinced that neither death nor life, neither angels nor demons, neither the present nor the future, nor any powers, neither height nor depth, nor anything else in all creation, will be able to separate us from the love of God that is in Christ Jesus our Lord. (Romans 8:28, 37–39, NIV)

CONTEMPLATION TOPIC 2:
CONTEMPLATING GRATITUDE

Next, we are going to focus on gratitude in contemplation. Start your time in silence and solitude by attending to your breathing, clearing your mind, and practicing stillness. Then you will have an opportunity to contemplate this topic's verse as well as *contemplating what you are grateful for right in that moment.*

When you contemplate what you are grateful for in the moment, please remember to incorporate the following:

- Be specific and detailed in your remembrance of blessings from others that come to mind.

- Consider things that surprised you that you are grateful for.

- Consider the temporal nature of the blessings you received—the reality that they could go away. Be thankful for them in light of that.

CONTEMPLATION FOCUS

Contemplate what you are grateful for right now, in this moment. Go with whatever comes to mind. If your mind wanders, just gently bring it back to this consideration.

Write down three things you are grateful for. Write in your journal, in a gratitude journal, or in something you will keep and can refer back to.

"Let the peace of Christ rule in your hearts, since as members of one body you were called to peace. And be thankful" (Colossians 3:15, NIV).

CONTEMPLATION TOPIC 3:
EXPRESSING GRATITUDE

Contemplate gratitude again, and take the time to express gratitude to someone in your life whom you appreciate.

CONTEMPLATION FOCUS

Consider the people in your life who have made the biggest difference for you in the past year. Choose the one who has been the most impactful. Spend time in contemplation considering that person's impact, and drill down in detail and depth regarding it.

Contact this person and set up a time to have a conversation with them expressing your gratitude in detail. If you can do it today, great. If not, set up a time to have the conversation.

Again, write down three things you are grateful for. Write in your journal, or in a gratitude journal, or in something you will keep and can refer back to.

> "*Let the message of Christ dwell among you richly as you teach and admonish one another with all wisdom through psalms, hymns, and songs from the Spirit, singing to God with gratitude in your hearts*" (Colossians 3:16, NIV).

CONTEMPLATION TOPIC 4:
JOURNALING ABOUT YOUR
EXPRESSION OF GRATITUDE

After your time in silence and solitude, stillness and contemplation, begin journaling about your expression of gratitude to the person you identified previously and talked to. If you have not talked to that person yet, then complete the journaling part of this topic when you have completed the conversation.

CONTEMPLATION FOCUS

Contemplate your experience during the gratitude conversation you had. Notice the feelings, physical sensations and experience you had during the conversation.

Journal about the conversation you had, expressing gratitude to the person you identified. Put the details of what occurred in your gratitude journal. Think about what occurred, how you felt, how you experienced the other person, the details of the other's response, and your thoughts after you were done. Write down any takeaways you have from the experience.

Again, write down three things you are grateful for. Write in your journal, or in a gratitude journal, or in something you will keep and can refer back to.

"And whatever you do, whether in word or deed, do it all in the name of the Lord Jesus, giving thanks to God the Father through him" (Colossians 3:17, NIV).

CONTEMPLATION TOPIC 5:
GRATITUDE FOR GOD AND HIS COMMUNITY

As always, begin with a time of stillness in silence and solitude. Clear your thoughts, attend to your breathing, and relax into the peace and presence of God.

CONTEMPLATION FOCUS

First contemplate the scripture below, and then contemplate with gratitude the amazing gift of being a part of God's community. Notice what comes to mind, and contemplate the aspects of his family that occur for you.

Again, write down three things you are grateful for. Write in your journal, or in a gratitude journal, or in something you will keep and can refer back to.

> *For this reason I kneel before the Father, from whom every family in heaven and on earth derives its name.*
>
> *I pray that out of his glorious riches he may strengthen you with power through his Spirit in your inner being, so that Christ may dwell in your hearts through faith.*
>
> *And I pray that you, being rooted and established in love, may have power, together with all the Lord's holy people, to grasp how wide and long and high and deep is the love of Christ, and to know this love that surpasses knowledge—that you may be filled to the measure of all the fullness of God.*
>
> *Now to him who is able to do immeasurably more than all we ask or imagine, according to his power that is at work within us, to him be glory in the church and in Christ Jesus throughout all generations, for ever and ever! Amen.* (Ephesians 3:14–21, NIV)

CHAPTER 10

STRATEGY FOR TRANSFORMATION

Throughout this study, we have covered the beginning disciplines of apprenticing with Jesus. Altogether, these constitute a strategy for inner and outer transformation, given by the One who called himself "the Way, the Truth, and the Life."

ENGAGING YOUR VISION

In the final chapter of this study, consider what area of your life you have the deepest desire to transform. Read this chapter with this specific area of your life in mind.

Perhaps no book in the New Testament introduces the concept and foundation of transformation better than the book of Romans. I often think of Romans as the Magna Carta of Christianity. The Magna Carta, written in 1215, was the first document in the history of England that listed the rights and powers of the people and was agreed to by the king. Romans, the first epistle to the church in the canon of the Bible, spells out our individual rights and powers as believers in Christ. It is a spiritual Magna Carta.

The first eight chapters of Romans go through the process of how we were redeemed and justified. This culminates in chapter 8, telling us that there is no condemnation in Christ, that we are more than conquerors, and that *nothing* can separate us from the love of God (Romans 8:31–39). The next two chapters are a parenthetical insertion regarding the status of Israel in relation to the Gentiles and the church, the body of Christ.

Finally, chapters 12 through the remainder of the book focus on how to practically walk out this new life we have been offered. They give us disciplines and practices to put into practice what we have been given by God as detailed in the first eight chapters. And chapter 12, as you know by now, starts with the central process we are called to: *transformation.*

TRANSFORMED BY THE RENEWING OF YOUR MIND

The beginning of Romans 12 lays out the strategy for transformation God has for us.

> Therefore, I urge you, brothers and sisters, in view of God's mercy, to offer your bodies as a living sacrifice, holy and pleasing to God—this is your true and proper worship.
>
> Do not conform to the pattern of this world, but be transformed by the renewing of your mind. Then you will be able to test and approve what God's will is—his good, pleasing and perfect will. (Romans 12:1–2, NIV)

As mentioned , the Greek word for "transformed" in this verse is transliterated into the word *metamorphosis* in English today. It basically means a complete change in form. In biology, the term is used to describe the change of a caterpillar to a pupa to an adult butterfly. Clearly, a butterfly looks nothing like the caterpillar or pupa it came from.

Essentially, *transformed* means brand-new—a whole new form. This Greek word is used four times in the New Testament. In Matthew 17:2 and Mark 9:2 it is translated "transfigured" when Jesus was transfigured before Peter, James, and John and his countenance completely changed so that he "shone before them" and his "clothes became as white as light." Its fourth and final usage is in 2 Corinthians 3:17–18, NIV:

> Now the Lord is the Spirit, and where the Spirit of the Lord is, there is freedom. And we all, who with unveiled faces contemplate (reflect) the Lord's glory, are being *transformed* into his image with ever-increasing glory, which comes from the Lord, who is the Spirit.

Read the previous verse again, while considering how this can literally be so for you in this life. It is a radical concept. The transformation

Paul talks about in Romans 12:2 means becoming a radically new being. New in action, new in heart, new in way of being, new in worldview. Our God is a God of *new*. He has promised a new creation (2 Corinthians 5:17), a new covenant (2 Corinthians 3:6), a new self (Ephesians 4:24), a new heart (Ezekiel 6:26), a new heaven (2 Peter 3:13), a new earth (2 Peter 3:13), a new song (Psalm 98:1), a new name (Revelation 2:17), a new spirit (Ezekiel 36:26), new wine and wineskin (Luke 5:36), and a new story (Revelation 21:5).

The culture we live in is not about new. It is about more, better, or different. Think about most advertising pitches and the entirety of the personal growth market today. They throw the word "transformation" around all the time. But, what they are usually referring to is not transformation—meaning brand new. It is about having more (more sex appeal, more money, more happiness) or about having it better (better looking, better health, better results) or about having it different (different friends, different beliefs, different results, different approach).

The problem with "more, better, different" is that it completely ties what you see possible in the moment to the past. To know whether something is more, better or different, you have to compare it to a historical standard in your life. So, what you consider possible in that moment is tied to what has occurred in your past. This is inherently limiting. It leads us to believe that we are our history, we are our story, and that we can't transcend our history. Yet, God is calling us to an entirely new story, an entirely new history.

God's game is not more, better, or different. God's game is brand new. That is what he is calling you to when he says you can be transformed.

The question is, "How do we create such radical newness in our life such that it is manifest in the real world?" We have covered this in many ways, but I will distill it down to the essentials here.

BECOMING RADICALLY NEW

There are three primary themes to becoming radically new. We explored the first two at the start of this study: living a lifestyle of repentance (changing your direction) and renewing our thought life (changing your thought life). Throughout the rest of this study, we continued to expound on these themes, while adding the third theme of transforming the posture of your heart.

Let's take a final brief look at each of these three themes.

1. LIFESTYLE OF REPENTANCE

A lifestyle of repentance means living responsibly, owning your own life and impact. It means you account for where you miss the mark. It means you recalibrate your trajectory when it gets off course and get back on the path again, and again, and again, and again.

Repentance is a lifestyle of openness and authenticity. The need for it never goes away because we are flawed and imperfect. Repentance is never about beating yourself up. That is indulgent selfishness. It is born out of godly sorrow for missing the mark with God and others. Repentance draws from gratitude that permeates the depths of your soul—a gratitude born when we realize the immensity of the gift of grace and mercy God has bestowed upon us with his invitation to eternal living and his gift of the new birth. Joy and delight are born from this depth of gratitude.

Repentance is the motivation for doing the disciplined work of renewing the mind, which includes renewing your thought life, renewing the posture of your heart, and renewing the impact you are having on the world on a continual basis.

Without embracing repentance as a lifestyle, you are unlikely to apprentice with Jesus for the long haul. *But as we said in the first week of this study, this is the true path to freedom and fulfillment. There is no other. This* is *the good life.*

2. RENEWING YOUR THOUGHT LIFE

The second foundational aspect of being transformed—living transformationally, becoming radically new—is renewing your thought life. With high-energy intentionality, as implied in 2 Corinthians 10:4–5, you demolish strongholds, demolish arguments and pretensions, and take thoughts captive. This is not the path of least resistance, and it does not necessarily come easily. But it is possible—it is doable!

God is challenging us to get in touch with the current reality of what is actually happening in our lives and to get busy renewing the thought patterns that are out of synch with God's truth and instead get busy building new thought patterns. To restate what we learned previously: Neuroscientists now know that humans can change their brains—they can build new neural pathways and establish new thought patterns. When we interrupt stronghold-based thought patterns and renew them into brand-new thought patterns based on the truth of what God says, we generate an entirely new way of relating that has a powerful impact on our experience of living. Doing so requires discipline, consistency, and a willingness to begin again and again, from a nonjudgmental, neutral, determined, and committed mind-set.

3. TRANSFORMING THE POSTURE OF YOUR HEART

The third and final aspect of transformation in this life is renewing and transforming the posture of your heart, including the parts of your life you are unaware of, yet work mischief in your life.

This is probably the aspect of transformation most missing in the church. It is very difficult to renew your thought life—the second aspect of transformation I mentioned—if the posture of your heart is not shifting. And, it is difficult to stick with the spiritual disciplines that support shifting the posture of your heart if you are not living repentance as a lifestyle. Owning the results of your life responsibly, rather than blaming yourself, someone else, or the circumstances are the foundation upon with new discipline and renewed vision is built. Recognizing the impact you have on others when you miss the mark of love is motivation to increase your will to embrace goodness in a fresh way.

Sometimes, even your best effort at renewing your conscious thought life does not take hold the way you would like. Sincere efforts can be undercut by underlying internal conversations—usually running in the background and limiting what you see possible in that moment.

These conversations are often rooted in scarcity themes like "I can't do this" or "I need this [insert whatever addictive behavior you struggle with] in order to get by" or in self-contempt beliefs like "I am not worth this." These conversations tend to run in the background of your mind—sometimes unconsciously, sometimes subconsciously, and sometimes consciously. They are part of the chatter in the back of your mind that just keeps running, all the time. They are part of the "way it is" for you. And no matter how much work you do to renew your conscious thoughts, these underlying limiting conversations don't go away.

Often these stuck areas of our life are tied to old wounds, raw spots in our hidden memories—rarely, if ever, thought of consciously. Just as often, they can be tied to events in our lives that we are aware of but that are unresolved, not fully mourned or forgiven.

The spiritual disciplines and prayer principles explored in this book are powerful paths toward renewing and transforming the posture of your heart. They allow God to do a deep work in your soul, based on his agenda rather than your own. When you are engaging silence, solitude, stillness, contemplation, and prayer, you are not setting up a specific point-by-point plan. You are disciplining yourself to simply be present, clearing extraneous thoughts, and noticing what you notice. You are resting in God's presence without an agenda. You are connecting to parts of your life that are normally under the waterline of your consciousness. You are noticing feelings, emotions, and senses that were before unknown to you. This is a rich environment for God to do his work.

For most of my adult life, I have been an impatient driver. I would get annoyed at other drivers if their behavior wasn't to my liking. I have been extremely self-aware of this for decades and have engaged in reframing my orientation literally thousands and thousands of times. And that brought me incremental improvement—maybe a twenty percent improvement at best. It was not until I embraced the disciplines of silence, solitude, stillness, contemplation, and contemplative prayer that I saw significant improvement in this area. I would say that at this point, I am at over a seventy percent improvement in being patient and calm when driving. I am thrilled.

How many times do you think I have contemplated this issue of my impatience in driving during my silence and solitude time? The answer is zero times. Never. Not once. That is the beauty of these disciplines. They allow an integration of heart, mind, and soul that enables God to do his work, in his way, on his schedule, and according to his agenda.

We get to surrender, practice acceptance, be with our imperfections without the felt need to eradicate them, and come along for the ride. Talk about an interruption to the hurried life! There is none better.

EMBRACING THE PROMISE OF HEAVEN NOW

In Philippians 1, Paul summarizes our commitment to live in the present out of a future worth having. One may ask, "If heaven is so great, why not just die now and be there?" There are two answers for that. First, to choose death over life is to spit in the face of all that Jesus accomplished for us. Second, it gives up our place of responsibility in the continuum of the development of God's heaven and earth and the kingdom of heaven. God's instruction is to always choose life.

> This day I call the heavens and the earth as witnesses against you that I have set before you life and death, blessings and curses. Now choose life, so that you and your children may live. (Deuteronomy 30:19, NIV)

Here is Paul's summary of why we embrace living now, anticipating the hope of heaven:

> For to me, to live is Christ and to die is gain. If I am to go on living in the body, this will mean fruitful labor for me. Yet what shall I choose? I do not know! I am torn between the two: I desire to depart and be with Christ, which is better by far; but it is more necessary for you that I remain in the body. Convinced of this, I know that I will remain, and I will continue with all of you for your progress and joy in the faith, so that through my being with you again, your boasting in Christ Jesus will abound on account of me. (Philippians 1:21–26, NIV)

We choose life here because we have work to do. We were saved and called for a purpose. We are in the restoration business along with our Father, God. It is the family business. If you think you are a nobody, you are sorely mistaken. You are called to be the essence of God's flavor for the world. You are the salt and the light of the world (Matthew 5:12–17).

You are participating in the kingdom of heaven, which is designed to grow in its influence in the world like a mustard seed grows and like yeast leavens bread (Matthew 13:31–34).

Your value lies in your identity in Christ (1 Corinthians 5:17, Galatians 2:20, Colossians 3:3, Romans 8:17), but you are a singularly unique expression of that identity (1 Corinthians 12:12–27). Your contribution matters.

You have a custom-designed destiny. You are called with a purpose. And you have complete freedom of will as to whether you embrace it or not. My deepest hope is that you embrace it, live it, and drink deeply of the fellowship of those immersed in the grace, mercy, goodness, and love of God. Delve deeply into the freeing power of God's forgiveness. Live in forgiveness and acceptance of others. Abide in overwhelming gratitude. Change the world.

Be the change the world so desperately craves. Work through the resistance you face—your own internal resistance and that of others. Stay the course of transforming your heart, your life, your relationships, your communities, and the world.

CONTINUING SPIRITUAL PRACTICES

Over the course of this study, we have engaged practicing stillness in various ways, and engaged many different forms of contemplation and contemplative prayer. We have also engaged various forms of conversational prayer.

Feel free to go back and pick up some of the spiritual practices you might have missed as you worked through this study. Or focus on the spiritual discipline practices you enjoyed the most. Enjoy your freedom to embrace our God with complete abandon, delight and devotion! What a gift of life we have been given. Enjoy!

NEXT STEPS

To discover free bonus resources for your *Apprenticing Jesus* study, visit:

https://KrisKile.com/ApprenticingJesusVideos

APPENDIX

APPRENTICING JESUS GROUP MEETING OUTLINES

Each group session starts with an OPENING ROUND where each person answers a series of statements, no more than 3 minutes each, up to 15-20 total minutes for all participants.

Then, as part of the CHAPTER DISCUSSION you will talk over each chapter's topics and daily practices, what you learned, and how you will apply it.

Finally, you will close the session with a FINAL CONNECTION ROUND, taking up to 3 minutes per person to assess your progress, which should take no longer than 15-20 minutes for everyone.

'RULES OF THE ROAD' AND GUIDELINES

Before the first session take 20 minutes to discuss the 'rules of the road' which will apply to all sessions. They are:

1. Take responsibility for what you learn and contribute

2. Speak authentically—be true to what is so for you—not at "The Truth" but as an authentic expression for the purpose of creating connection.

3. Maintain confidentiality

Then, go over these guidelines:

1. If you are going to be late or absent, call or text someone.

2. No cell phone use during the meeting, unless permission is asked at the beginning of the meeting.

3. If you decide to leave the group before the study is complete, have a conversation with someone from the group.

SESSION ONE:
YOUR RESPONSE TO AN INVITATION OF A LIFETIME

(15-20 MINUTES)

OPENING ROUND

For the opening round, each person answers the following statement, after greeting the others:

What I hope to gain from my participation in this *Apprenticing Jesus* study is...

(30 MINUTES)

CHAPTER DISCUSSION

Group discussion about the CHAPTER 1 of *Apprenticing Jesus* with conversation about your vision for this *Apprenticing Jesus* group study journey.

(15-20 MINUTES)

FINAL CONNECTION ROUND

Answer one or more of the following statements:

- What opened up for me during this meeting is...
- What I am discovering is...
- How this activity and/or discussion impacted me is...
- What I am learning is...
- What I am experiencing or feeling is...
- What I want to work on, moving forward is...

Close with prayer.

SESSION TWO:
BEGINNING STEPS AS AN APPRENTICE

(15-20 MINUTES)

OPENING ROUND

For the opening round, each person answers the following check in statements, after greeting the others:

- Right now, on a scale of 1 (struggling) to 10 (feeling great), I am…

- One thing I am excited about is…

- One thing I am concerned about…

- One thing I am curious about…

(10 MINUTES)

INTERACTIVE EXERCISE—VISION AND OWNING YOUR EXPERIENCE

Pair up with someone you don't know well in the group. If there are an odd number of people, do one group of three and apportion the time so everyone can speak.

Do a two-way sharing exercise answering the question:

"What I want to create from my involvement in this small group over during this study is…." (Both go at once, each shares. Time it.)

Focus on using "I" statements in this (instead of "we" or "you" statements) and establish this as a discipline for the entire group all the time. "I" statements are designed to invite us to "own my life."

(40 MINUTES)

CHAPTER DISCUSSION

Group discussion about CHAPTER 2: BEGINNING STEPS AS AN APPRENTICE, with conversation about the daily practices at the end of CHAPTER 2. Discuss what you learned regarding the process of repentance.

(15-20 MINUTES)

FINAL CONNECTION ROUND

Answer one or more of the following statements:

- What opened up for me during this meeting is…
- What I am discovering is…
- How this activity and/or discussion impacted me is…
- What I am learning is…
- What I am experiencing or feeling is…
- What I want to work on, moving forward is…

Close with prayer.

SESSION THREE:
JESUS AND THE PRACTICE OF SILENCE AND SOLITUDE

(15-20 MINUTES)

OPENING ROUND

For the opening round, each person answers the following check in statements, after greeting the others:

- Right now, on a scale of 1 (struggling) to 10 (feeling great), I am...

- One thing I am excited about is...

- One thing I am concerned about is...

- One thing I am curious about is...

(40 MINUTES)

CHAPTER DISCUSSION

Group discussion about CHAPTER 3: JESUS AND THE PRACTICE OF SILENCE AND SOLITUDE, with conversation about how everyone is doing with the daily spiritual practices on pages at the end of the chapter.

Spend some time on discussing the nature and condition of your prayer life. Where do you desire more intimacy in your walk with God? How would that impact the areas in your life where you are currently struggling?

(6 MINUTES)

INTERACTIVE EXERCISE—SHARING EXERCISE

Pair up with someone in the group you haven't paired with. If there are an odd number of people, do one group of three and apportion the time so everyone can speak.

Answer this sentence stem in your sharing with your partner for this exercise:

The key areas I desire more intimacy in my walk with God and how that would impact my life is...

(15-20 MINUTES)

FINAL CONNECTION ROUND

Answer one or more of the following statements:

- What opened up for me during this meeting is…

- What I am discovering is…

- How this activity and/or discussion impacted me is…

- What I am learning is…

- What I am experiencing or feeling is…

- What I want to work on, moving forward is…

Close with prayer.

SESSION FOUR:
THE UNHURRIED LIFE: MERGING & EMERGING

(15-20 MINUTES)

OPENING ROUND

For the opening round, each person answers the following check in statements, after greeting the others:

- Right now, on a scale of 1 (struggling) to 10 (feeling great), I am...
- One thing I am excited about is...
- One thing I am concerned about is...
- One thing I am curious about is...

(40 MINUTES)

CHAPTER DISCUSSION

Group discussion about CHAPTER 4: THE UNHURRIED LIFE: MERGING AND EMERGING, with conversation about how everyone is doing with the daily spiritual practices at the end of the chapter. During your discussion, spend some time discussing your answers to this consideration: consider the impact busyness and hurry Is having on your life... what impact could practicing rest and stillness have on your life and relationships?

(15-20 MINUTES)

FINAL CONNECTION ROUND

Answer one or more of the following statements:

- What opened up for me during this meeting is...
- What I am discovering is...
- How this activity and/or discussion impacted me is..
- What I am learning is...
- What I am experiencing or feeling is...
- What I want to work on, moving forward is....

Close with prayer.

SESSION FIVE:
COMMUNING WITH GOD

(15-20 MINUTES)

OPENING ROUND

For the opening round, each person answers the following check in statements, after greeting the others:

- Right now, on a scale of 1 (struggling) to 10 (feeling great), I am...

- One thing I am excited about is...

- One thing I am concerned about is...

- One thing I am curious about is...

(40 MINUTES)

CHAPTER DISCUSSION

Group discussion about CHAPTER 5: COMMUNING WITH GOD, with conversation about what you discovered and considered regarding your prayer life when reading this chapter. Discuss the power of the Apprentice's (Lord's) prayer as an expression of faith and trust in God.

(15-20 MINUTES)

FINAL CONNECTION ROUND

Answer one or more of the following statements:

- What opened up for me during this meeting is...

- What I am discovering is...

- How this activity and/or discussion impacted me is...

- What I am learning is...

- What I am experiencing or feeling is...

- What I want to work on, moving forward is...

Close with prayer.

SESSION SIX:
THE HEART OF APPRENTICESHIP

(15-20 MINUTES)

OPENING ROUND

For the opening round, each person answers the following check in statements, after greeting each other:

- Right now, on a scale of 1 (struggling) to 10 (feeling great), I am…
- One thing I am excited about is…
- One thing I am concerned about is…
- One thing I am curious about is…

(40 MINUTES)

CHAPTER DISCUSSION

Group discussion about CHAPTER 6: THE HEART OF APPRENTICESHIP, with conversation about how everyone is doing with the daily spiritual practices at the end of the chapter.

Spend some time discussing which aspect of your declared vision for this ten-week time frame is currently stuck. Discuss what requests you can make to God that will start a conversation about what is wanted and needed in that situation.

(6 MINUTES)

INTERACTIVE EXERCISE—SHARING EXERCISE

Pair up with someone in the group for this sharing exercise. If there are an odd number of people, do one group of three and apportion the time so everyone can speak.

Answer these sentence stems in your sharing with your partner for this exercise:

The areas of my vision that are currently not moving as much as desire are…

The requests I see I can make to God to invite him into this challenge are…

(15-20 MINUTES)

FINAL CONNECTION ROUND

Answer one or more of the following statements:

- What opened up for me during this meeting is...

- What I am discovering is...

- How this activity and/or discussion impacted me is...

- What I am learning is...

- What I am experiencing or feeling is...

- What I want to work on, moving forward is...

Close with prayer.

SESSION SEVEN:
THE SPIRITUAL PRACTICE OF AUTHENTICITY

(15-20 MINUTES)

OPENING ROUND

For the opening round, each person answers the following check in statements, after greeting the others:

- Right now, on a scale of 1 (struggling) to 10 (feeling great), I am…

- One thing I am excited about is…

- One thing I am concerned about is…

- One thing I am curious about is…

(40 MINUTES)

CHAPTER DISCUSSION

Group discussion about CHAPTER 7: THE SPIRITUAL PRACTICE OF AUTHENTICITY, with conversation about how everyone is doing with the daily spiritual practices oat the end of the chapter.

Spend some time on discussing where you can lean into being more authentic in your life, and what gets in the way of being true to what is so for you. Consider and discuss how this is impacting your vision for this *Apprenticing Jesus* journey.

(6 MINUTES)

INTERACTIVE EXERCISE—SHARING EXERCISE

Pair up with someone in the group for this exercise. If there are an odd number of people, do one group of three and apportion the time so everyone can speak.

Answer these sentence stems in your sharing with your partner for this exercise.

Where I notice I am being less than fully authentic is…

My commitment to lean into authenticity includes…

(15-20 MINUTES)

FINAL CONNECTION ROUND

Answer one or more of the following statements:

- What opened up for me during this meeting is...

- What I am discovering is...

- How this activity and/or discussion impacted me is...

- What I am learning is...

- What I am experiencing or feeling is...

- What I want to work on, moving forward is...

Close with prayer.

SESSION EIGHT:
FORGIVENESS, THE FOUNDATION OF FREEDOM

(15-20 MINUTES)

OPENING ROUND

For the opening round, each person answers the following check in statements, after greeting the others:

- Right now, on a scale of 1 (struggling) to 10 (feeling great), I am...
- One thing I am excited about is...
- One thing I am concerned about is...
- One thing I am curious about is...

(40 MINUTES)

CHAPTER DISCUSSION

Group discussion about CHAPTER 8: FORGIVENESS, THE FOUNDATION OF FREEDOM, with conversation about how everyone is doing with the daily spiritual practices at the end of the chapter.

Spend some time discussing where you can embrace forgiveness in your life. Where do you still carry hurt, disappointment, and judgment? Where do you notice you have more work to do? Discuss the areas you desire to engage this further.

(6 MINUTES)

INTERACTIVE EXERCISE—SHARING EXERCISE

Pair up with someone in the group for this exercise. If there are an odd number of people, do one group of three and apportion the time so everyone can speak.

Answer these sentence stems in your sharing with your partner for this exercise:

Where I notice I have additional forgiveness to extend in my life is...

What I am going to do to embrace this is...

(15-20 MINUTES)

FINAL CONNECTION ROUND

Answer one or more of the following statements:

- What opened up for me during this meeting is…
- What I am discovering is…
- How this activity and/or discussion impacted me is…
- What I am learning is…
- What I am experiencing or feeling is…
- What I want to work on, moving forward is…

Close with prayer.

SESSION NINE:
PEACE AND GRATITUDE

(15-20 MINUTES)

OPENING ROUND

For the opening round, each person answers the following check in statements, after greeting the others:

- Right now, on a scale of 1 (struggling) to 10 (feeling great), I am...
- One thing I am excited about is...
- One thing I am concerned about is...
- One thing I am curious about is...

(40 MINUTES)

CHAPTER DISCUSSION

Group discussion about CHAPTER 9: PEACE AND GRATITUDE, with conversation about how everyone is doing with the daily spiritual practices at the end of the chapter.

Spend some time on discussing where you can embrace gratitude in your life, especially relative to the current challenges you are experiencing. Where do notice that embracing gratitude can propel you forward?

(6 MINUTES)

INTERACTIVE EXERCISE—SHARING EXERCISE

Pair up with someone in the group you haven't paired with. If there are an odd number of people, do one group of three and apportion the time so everyone can speak.

Answer these sentence stems in your sharing with your partner for this exercise.

The areas I need to practice gratitude in are...

The attitudes I will need to release in order to do this are...

(15-20 MINUTES)

FINAL CONNECTION ROUND

Answer one or more of the following statements:

- What opened up for me during this meeting is...

- What I am discovering is...

- How this activity and/or discussion impacted me is...

- What I am learning is...

- What I am experiencing or feeling is...

- What I want to work on, moving forward is...

Close with prayer.

SESSION TEN:
STRATEGY FOR TRANSFORMATION

(15-20 MINUTES)

OPENING ROUND

For the opening round, each person answers the following check in statements, after greeting the others:

- Right now, on a scale of 1 (struggling) to 10 (feeling great), I am...
- One thing I am excited about is...
- One thing I am concerned about is...
- One thing I am curious about is...

(40 MINUTES)

CHAPTER DISCUSSION

Group discussion about CHAPTER 10: STRATEGY FOR TRANSFORMATION, with conversation about conversation about how everyone is doing with the daily spiritual practices at the end of the chapter.

Spend some time discussing the area of your life you have the deepest desire to transform. Discuss what you are noticing about what will support you in spiritual growth in that area.

(6 MINUTES)

INTERACTIVE EXERCISE—SHARING EXERCISE

Pair up with someone in the group you haven't paired with. If there are an odd number of people, do one group of three and apportion the time so everyone can speak.

Answer these sentence stems in your sharing with your partner for this exercise.

Moving forward, the area of my life I have the deepest desire to transform...

My next steps toward growth in this are...

(15-20 MINUTES)

FINAL CONNECTION ROUND

Answer one or more of the following statements:

- What opened up for me during this meeting is...

- What I am discovering is...

- How this activity and/or discussion impacted me is...

- What I am learning is...

- What I am experiencing or feeling is...

- What I want to work on, moving forward is...

Close with prayer.

REFERENCES

[1] Henri Nouwen, *Spiritual Formation: Following the Movements of the Spirit* (New York: HarperOne Reprint edition, 2010).

[2] E. W. Bullinger, "Repentance", *A Critical Lexicon and Concordance to the English and Greek New Testament* (Grand Rapids, MI: Kregel Publications, 1999), 688.

[3] "Catholic News, Commentary, Information, Resources, and the Liturgical Year," Catholic Culture, Accessed February 13, 2019, http://www.catholicculture.org.

[4] Michael Casey OCSO, *The Road to Eternal Life* (Collegeville, MN: Liturgical Press, 2012).

[5] "Virtue," *Wikipedia*, February 06, 2019, Accessed February 13, 2019, https://en.wikipedia.org/wiki/Virtue.

[6] E. W. Bullinger, "Sin", *A Critical Lexicon and Concordance to the English and Greek New Testament* (Grand Rapids, MI: Kregel Publications, 1999), 703.

[7] Dallas Willard, *The Divine Conspiracy: Rediscovering Our Hidden Life in God* (New York: HarperOne, 2018), 353.

[8] Henri Nouwen, Henri J. M. *The Way of the Heart* (New York: Ballantine Books, 2003), 25.

[9] Ibid., 27-28.

[10] John Eldredge, *Desire: The Journey We Must Take to Find the Life God Offers* (Nashville: Thomas Nelson, 2007).

[11] Ibid., 43.

[12] John Ortberg, *The Life You've Always Wanted*, 76.

[13] E. W. Bullinger, *A Critical Lexicon and Concordance to the English and Greek New Testament* (Grand Rapids, MI: Kregel Publications, 1999), 95.

[14] Ibid. 862.

[15] Ibid. 642.

[16] Ibid. 317.

[17] Ibid. 389.

[18] Ibid. 362.

[19] A yoke literally was a bar of wood, constructed to join together two animals (usually oxen), enabling them to work in the fields, drawing loads, and pulling farm instruments. It was a metaphor for bearing a burden.

[20] E. W. Bullinger, *A Critical Lexicon and Concordance to the English and Greek New Testament* (Grand Rapids, MI: Kregel Publications, 1999), 243.

[21] Ibid. 456.

[22] Ibid. 447.

[23] Ibid. 434.

[24] Thomas Keating, *Intimacy With God*, 1.

[25] "This translation of John 1:1-14 was translated by Biblical Greek scholar, Clive Scott, at the encouragement of his friend, David Moore, in 2001, using Erasmus's translation of the word "conversation" instead of the word "word" as the English translation of the Greek word "logos." Clive's comments regarding this translation follow:

"These notes were attached to the first copy of the 'Logos as Conversation' text.

John 1. 1-14 'The Introduction'

"I can hear some people saying that this is a paraphrase and not a translation. But I would dispute that. A paraphrase in this context is a 'filling out' of the traditional interpretation (translation) to try and cope with the transition from the Greek of the traditional interpretation into English. But this is not what I have attempted to do here. I have taken the premise that logos is to be understood as 'conversation' and then listened to the Greek in the light of that. It puts a different slant on everything. If the original readers heard 'conversation', what would they then go on to hear? Now put that into English. That is translation.

The first translators into English heard the Church Fathers (and their Greek Philosophy), and put that into English, most translations, if not all, build on that. We value the translation 'Logos as Word', because that dealt with the Jewish/Greek listening. The two translations need to be heard in stereo! I still think that these verses begin and end the introduction, and that everything which follows is the story which unpacks this introduction.

There are lots of things that I have heard in a new way. Using the idea of 'conversation' gives much more of the sense of things 'going on' to those first verses ... activity, harmony not unison, i.e. life. THIS was the life, this God mobility, this interaction which IS God. Quite a movement away from the Ian Paisley figure who speaks the WORD and it all happens. And so, if it is this mobility, the collaboration, this conversation, which is the life THEN IT IS THAT NATURE OF LIFE WHICH IS REVEALED AND IN WHICH WE CAN SHARE. This, being the introduction, has implication for the whole Gospel story. One would like to go on and translate the whole Gospel with this in mind.

There are a lot of things I have enjoyed discovering in this exercise. There is a wholeness about this passage which is often lost in our translations. The verses usually come out as a series of disconnected statements, but it is a very subtle whole, all linked together by words which carry the reader from one stage to the next. I have tried to capture that.

I liked using 'observe' because it captures the sense of 'see and do', 'perceive and follow', 'have faith and be a disciple', even though it sits rather uncomfortably at the end of the sentence in paragraph 2.

At the end, the use of the cliché 'a glorious opportunity not to be missed' cried out to be dismissed until one asks how else do you express 'grace upon grace' not to be heard as a Reformation theological statement, but as a response of wonder from those who got the message, saw the point, shared the life, grasped it, had faith i.e. perceived and joined in?

'The nature of life' is also a cliché phrase and you might have your own suggestion. But some other phrase must express the point that it is just that nature, the sort of life on offer, that concerns John. That is the subject of the introduction, and indeed the subject of the whole Gospel. The remarkable thing, the 'grace upon grace' is the astonishing call for us to be co-creators. This is where *Introduction* ends.

Verse 15. 'The Gospel now begins!'

Thinking about the ways of hearing the word 'witness' in verse 15, confirms my hunch about logos as conversation.

If the subject is 'conversation' then one hears 'witness' not just as a pointer 'Gosh, look at that', but as an inviter, 'here it is, share it.' One joins a conversation but not a proclamation. At the heart of the Gospel there is always an invitation to join in, that is the Good News."

Clive Scott Colloquy ©

[26] Martin Heidegger, *Letter on Humanism.*

[27] Marciano Guerrero, "Title," January 12, 2012, www.writingtolive.com.

[28] Richard Rohr, *The Naked Now*, 89.

[29] Chambers, Oswald, *My Utmost For His Highest.*

[30] Martin Luther King, Jr. *Strength To Love* (London: Fount, 1977), 47-48, 51-52. Adapted to inclusive language.

[31] Ibid., 48, 54-55. Adapted to inclusive language.

[32] Thomas Keating, *The Human Condition.*

[33] American Psychological Association Study, 2007.

[34] American Institute of Stress, NY.

[35] "The Economic Burden of Anxiety Disorders", a study commissioned by ADAA *The Journal of Clinical Psychiatry*, 60(7), July 1999.

[36] Anxiety and Depression Association of America.

[37] August 2013 survey by Harris Interactive for the American Psychological Association.

[38] Ibid.

[39] Ibid.

[40] E. W. Bullinger, *A Critical Lexicon and Concordance to the English and Greek New Testament* (Grand Rapids, MI: Kregel Publications, 1999).

[41] Robert Emmons, *Gratitude Works!*, Jossey-Bass, v-vi.

[42] Ibid., 9, 10.

[43] Ibid., 81.

[44] E. W. Bullinger, *A Critical Lexicon and Concordance to the English and Greek New Testament* (Grand Rapids, MI: Kregel Publications, 1999).

[45] Ibid, 45.

Made in the USA
Coppell, TX
10 December 2021

67987524R00115